THE POWER OF
THE PALATE

Thank you Lauren!

THE POWER OF THE PALATE

THROUGH THE GREAT EXCHANGE

Kathiana LeJeune

KATHIANA LEJEUNE

NEW DEGREE PRESS

COPYRIGHT © 2020 KATHIANA LEJEUNE

THE POWER OF THE PALATE
Through the Great Exchange

ISBN	978-1-63676-589-1	*Paperback*
	978-1-63676-224-1	*Kindle Ebook*
	978-1-63676-225-8	*Ebook*

To Momma, My Late Grams, and Late Papa Ben,

Thank you for the sacrifices that you all have made for Millie and me and allowing me to grow to have an open mind and a heart to serve others.

To Millie

Thank you for being such a supportive little sister and cheering me on along the way! Love you!

CONTENTS

INTRODUCTION: THE POWER OF THE PALATE THROUGH THE GREAT EXCHANGE

Do you enjoy wining and dining?

Have you ever had a meal that you enjoyed and thought everyone should try?

Has a meal ever made you feel better?

Or has pop culture helped you title yourself as a foodie?

For those who don't know foodie means *a person who loves food and is very interested in different types of food.*[1] Julia Child said it best that "People who love to eat are always the

1   *The Cambridge English Dictionary*, s.v. "foodie (n.)," 2020.

best people."[2] What makes the two so great, food and people, is that a mutual love of food can bring different people together.

When we sit back and think, no matter who you are or what you believe in, everyone can agree that our world matters and what fuels our souls aside from religion is *food*. Every culture embodies a way of food preparation or a part of them that goes into the pot. As we travel and experience new food through food introductions, a term called *ubuntu* begins to happen through food, flavor, and exchanging a meal. The term ubuntu means "I am because you are, and you are because I am." Our world infuses culture through food introductions throughout our various countries, cities, and states. We often encounter these introductions through travel, simple weekend escapes, trying out new restaurants, dinners at a friend's home, or through the curiosity of trying new recipes. Food plays a huge role in our cultural identity, traditions, relationships, and overall human connections. Our palates—taste buds or outlook of other cultures—amplify and strengthen throughout one of the greatest exchanges we can have, sharing a good meal and having a meaningful conversation.

John F. Kennedy said it best that "Food is strength, and food is peace, and food **is freedom, and** food **is a helping hand to people around the world whose goodwill and friendship we**

---

2   "A Quote by Julia Child," Goodreads.com, 2020.

want.[3] Throughout this book, I will share instances of diplomats, everyday travelers, non-government organizations, and people who have expanded their perception and acceptance of other cultures through food introductions. Moreover, through these food introductions and dinners, they expand their relationships, business opportunities, friendships, and new travel experiences. So, why not use this for peace talks and conflict resolution?

I recently had the opportunity to speak with my former colleague and friend Veaceslav Pituscan, Former Moldova Ambassador. He told me how the various state dinners he has attended have changed some policy's status not only because of the discussions that took place but also because of the opportunity to wine and dine with other diplomats.

He expressed how one of the dinners brought him closer to a Ukrainian ambassador due to a bread called Mamaliga being served at the dinner. He explained to me briefly about Ukraine and Moldova's history and how Mamaliga dates back as far as the 16th century and how it has migrated through the Eastern European culture. I found it interesting how various foods and cultural backgrounds could bring us together. Veaceslav expressed how the exchange of Mamaliga was an instance of food diplomacy, for it helped with the conversations they had with Ukraine about some of the policy differences they had at the time. He said, "Me and the Ukrainian ambassador instantly connected over Mamaliga because it reminded me of my home and him of his."

---

3   John F. Kennedy, Pre-Presidential Papers, "Remarks at Corn Palace in Mitchell, South Dakota." September 22, 1960.

After this conversation with Veaceslav, I felt the urge to take a look at how food can be a new form of diplomacy. For if the best way to a man or woman's heart is through food, how that can dull the edge of a sharp sword and soothe a conversation is an actual thing that no one has really talked about. I found that various statesmen, diplomats, and embassies host working dinners to aid in conversations about an initiative or to negotiate policy. This reminds me of Albert Einstein's quote of when he once said that "Peace cannot be kept by force. It can only be achieved by understanding," and in this book I plan on expanding on how food plays a vital role in achieving peace through understanding each other through meal exchanges.

I plan on taking a quick look at how food plays a vast role in understanding through human culture. Throughout my research, I came across a nonprofit company called Global Gastros, who did a study on how food plays a role in human culture. I found it interesting how they analyzed the differences of humankind through food. I remember reading an article by Global Gastros, "The Role of Food in Human Culture." The article mentions *how* "our minds have allowed us to develop civilization, create incredible technology, and literally change the face of our planet. With all the advances of the human race, we often forget that our uniqueness throughout earth goes back even further and deeper, back to the very roots of our existence and to one of our most basic needs—food."[4]

---

4   "The Role of Food in Human Culture," Global Gastros, 2018.

They went on to express how we as people have an emotional connection with food before having an instinctive need for food—meaning that it goes beyond being hangry sometimes, for food can be love, memory, connection, and understanding and that is what strengthens us as people, no matter your roots. To look into the concept of emotional connections through food is looking at travel and one's motive to travel. One of my favorite things throughout this writing process is that during my interviews with colleagues, former professors, and friends, I ask them what fuels their passions for travel and experiencing other cultures. One of the top answers that I hear is the opportunity to try new foods that are different than what they are used to eating or their overall dining experience.

Personally, I enjoy traveling because it allows me a chance to see another side of the world. I too love getting the opportunity to try new foods and dining cultures. I also enjoy getting to see landmarks, historical sites, beaches, and other excursions that are meaningful to the nation and people that I visit. What fuels this passion for food, travel, and culture is my family's background.

So, my family is originally from Haiti. Growing up, we would go to Haiti almost every summer for two weeks and have a blast every time. What makes my experience there so unique, aside from understanding and speaking Haitian Creole, was the food. The preparation and bond that goes into creating the amazing dishes is what I appreciated most. From the people at the market, bargaining, to the freshness of the food and the gossip that goes on in the kitchen while preparing the food, it all makes the experience more enjoyable when sitting around the table or TV watching soccer.

Oftentimes in our societies, we miss out on spending time with others due to the busyness of our schedules, difference in language, food preferences options, or *introvertedness.* Because our culture is reliant on food and having human connections and relationships through meals, we value the beauty of sharing a meal with one another.

Our palates become more powerful during our great meal exchanges throughout life. I know that throughout my dining experiences both in the States with family and friends and internationally, a remarkable meal has always allowed my interest to spark about the culture or the people who prepared the food. Maybe it's my obsession for cooking and baking or because of my desire to learn about other cultures. Either way, I always find myself willing to try to cook these meals or find restaurants in my city that resemble a similar flavor of the dish that I had during my travels or meals at a friend's home. I often find myself inviting friends or my roommates to join me during this dinner and to just enjoy meals from different cuisines and catch up. I plan on discussing this more in a future chapter, but the atmosphere of my living/dining room area and flavor of the food is what I aim at replicating to see if I can make it a nostalgic moment for myself and a new experience for those that I invite to take part in this experience.

The title of my book, *The Power of the Palate through the Great Exchange*, comes from the diverse meaning or perspective of the word "palate." The word "palate" means the roof of the mouth, separating the cavities of the nose and the mouth in vertebrates. It also means a person's appreciation of taste and flavor, especially when sophisticated and discriminating. Some also define it as shades, art, taste. One of my colleagues at *National Geographic*, Chad Sandus, Vice President of Talent, shared that the first thing that comes to mind when hearing the word palate is an artist's palette and our own personal palates. He expressed how we have developed our palate through what have we been able to sample over time. He says that "I think people's palates deepen over time because they have more life experience, more travel experience, or more food experience." Oftentimes, our palate grows based on memory, like a "great taste from the past."

What I loved most during this interview and many others is how everyone notices how powerful our palates are and how they can shift perspective, perception, and persuasions of trying new foods, exploring other cultures, and understanding one another. Join me through the pages of this book to navigate how our palate becomes more powerful through life's greatest exchange—a meal and conversation at the dinner table that is meaningful, shifts perspective, and aids in power. Food is the new form of diplomacy; now let's talk.

I

1

CONNECTING THROUGH FOOD

———

Eating is so intimate. It's very sensual. When you invite some-
one to sit at your table and you want to cook for them, you're
inviting a person into your life.

—MAYA ANGELOU[5]

Our connections with each other are often formed through exchanging a meal. Food has that power to bring us together and silence the invisible borders of our differences, all while appreciating the flavors of a dish. We share laughter, stories, and sometimes tears during our wine-and-dines with one another. We often enjoy having company over and enjoying a delicious dish. When we engage in our human connections like sharing a meal or connecting through food, we not only fuel our bodies, but we also fuel our souls through the conversations that take place. Friendships, partnerships,

---

5   Maya Angelou, "BrainyQuote.com," *BrainyMedia, Inc.,* 2020.

business opportunities, and other deep relationships stem from those very moments, along with memories that form and stick with you for a lifetime regardless if you ponder over those moments or not.

Personally, I am a true foodie, and nothing gets me more excited than trying a new recipe, restaurant, food truck, or dinner at one of my friends' homes. Those moments and encounters are ones that have a special place in my heart, and memory of a good time allows me to share stories with those who are both directly and indirectly related to those encounters. Throughout my student leadership ice-breaker experiences, one of the top three questions I would ask my group or team would be:

1. If you could be an animal, what animal would you be and why?
2. What is your favorite dish and why?
3. What is your favorite season (fall, winter, spring, and summer) and most memorable pastime within that season?

My favorite responses would come from questions number two and three. Oftentimes, the stories of the various individuals would be connected in a unique way; for example, when I served as the Senator of Clubs and Organizations at Georgia State University Perimeter College at the Clarkston Campus, I would have strategy sessions to increase the visibility and collaboration opportunities amongst the clubs. What I had noticed during these sessions was the differences amongst both the student leaders and their clubs. The Clarkston campus was very diverse, and it was both captivating and interesting to hear the perspectives of most students especially during the ice breakers. Before our first strategy session began, I had them sit in a huge circle and tell the group what their favorite season was and their most memorable pastime. The answers all varied because not everyone was from the US, but most of the students answered summer or fall and everyone's pastime included camping, swimming, enjoying the beach, or going to parties or barbecues. During one of the sessions, I noticed that everyone had a version of enjoying a barbecue regardless of the season. Some said Fourth of July barbecue, fall campfire s'mores or wieners on a campfire, winter Canadian barbecue, or springtime gatherings with barbecued kabobs. I kid you not that in a group of twenty-five people over fifteen responses included barbecue.

CONCEPT OF BREAKING BREAD

Now looking back, I realize that there is a true connection between people and our relationship with food. I was reading an article that described the uniqueness of our relationship to food:

> From our ancestors first cooking food to today where we are literally changing food on a molecular level. Beyond the technological relationship we have with food, humans are also unique in our emotional connection with food. In the rest of the animal kingdom, food is by and large simply a matter of providing nutrients to one's body. Animals eat out of instinct. Humans, on the other hand, see food as so much more than just a nutritional need. In fact, we often use food in a destructive way—overeating and eating

*unhealthy foods—which negatively impacts our bod-
ies instead. For humans, food seems to sit on an emotional level first before being an instinctive need. The
answer lies in humankind's deep connection with
food. It is not just about mindless eating—it is about
preparing, creating, discovering, exploring, inventing,
and changing our food and food landscape.*[6]

Moreover, it is in our relationship with food that oftentimes
we are able to connect with others. The concept of human
connection is an energy exchange between people who are
paying attention to one another. It has the power to *deepen
the moment, inspire change, and build trust.* I truly believe
that this is how the concept of breaking bread came to be
after Christ did it.

If anyone is like my older cousins Arie or Oprah, I know, you
love bread! I personally enjoy making breads with fillers, for
example: pumpkin chocolate chip, blueberry lemon, lemon
and lavender, rosemary and garlic, orange and cranberry,
and banana breads.

However, I never get the satisfaction of trying and eating the
entire loaf alone. I personally am happy when I get to share
my bakes with others, and everyone on the receiving end
of my bakes can agree that it makes them happy as well. I'll
never forget bringing in my pumpkin chocolate chip bread
the same day as a possible stakeholder for a company that I
worked for came in and tried a slice. Prior to meeting with
the board, he made a point to tell me that my bread was

6   "The Role of Food in Human Culture," *Global Gastros*, 2018.

probably one of the most delicious sweet breads that he had tried and could not believe how he didn't need coffee to complement it and how it stood on its own and how I missed my calling. He also expressed his baking experiences and was trying to guess what my secret was. He told me that while he hadn't signed official paperwork that if he were to join our team, he would love to have a bake off. I was on cloud nine and was happy I was not only able to share it with my team and other staff but also, I was able to win the heart of our stakeholder. At that moment, we had a connection through food. We were able to literally break bread and connect on something that was beyond business.

PUMPKIN BREAD RECIPE

INGREDIENTS:
- 1 1/2 cups all-purpose flour, plus more for coating chocolate chips
- 1 teaspoon homemade (recipe below) or store-bought pumpkin pie spice
- 1/4 teaspoon salt
- 1/2 teaspoon baking soda
- 1 cup granulated sugar
- 1 cup pumpkin puree
- 3/4 cup avocado oil (you can use vegetable oil if you don't have avocado oil)
- 2 eggs
- 1/2 teaspoon vanilla extract
- 1 1/4 cups semisweet chocolate chips divided
- PAM non-stick spray

INSTRUCTIONS:

Preheat the oven to 350 F. Coat an 8 x 4-inch loaf pan with PAM non-stick spray.

Place the flour, pumpkin pie spice, salt and baking soda in a large bowl; whisk to combine.

Add the sugar, pumpkin puree, avocado oil, eggs and vanilla extract to the flour mixture. Stir until just combined.

Toss 1 cup of the chocolate chips with 1 tablespoon flour (This helps the chocolate chips not sink to the bottom of the mixture once it's in the oven). Stir the chocolate chips into the batter.

Pour the batter into the prepared pan. Sprinkle the remaining 1/4 cup chocolate chips over the top of the loaf.

Bake for 55-65 minutes or until a toothpick inserted into the center of the loaf comes out clean. Cool for 10 minutes, then run a thin knife along the sides of the pan to loosen the bread.

Let the bread cool in the pan, then invert, slice and serve.

PUMPKIN SPICE INGREDIENTS:
- 3 tablespoons ground cinnamon
- 2 teaspoons ground ginger
- 2 teaspoons nutmeg
- 1 ½ teaspoons ground allspice
- 1 ½ teaspoons ground cloves

* * *

At this moment I noticed that concept of breaking bread has multiple meanings. While the main meaning is the of sharing a meal with someone, it has evolved into something that means more than just eating; it is sharing a sense of sisterhood or brotherhood with someone or a group of people. It is a significant event that fosters some meaningful connection and cooperation. Even if you are enemies with someone, if you break bread with them it indicates or symbolizes a sense of forgiveness and moving forward.

Within the concept of breaking bread there is a point for a social connection to be made. When researchers refer to the concept of "social connection," they mean the feeling that you belong to a group and generally feel close to other people. Scientific evidence strongly suggests that this is a core psychological need essential to feeling satisfied with your life. The funny thing about this is that our best moments are often through sharing a meal. Food becomes this catalyst in both our human connection and social connection and becomes more than just enjoy what's on your plate but often times the conversations or the relationships that are formed through these encounters.

HISTORY NUGGETS AND HOSPITALITY BITES

I'll never forget my friend Veaceslav telling me about his encounter with a Ukrainian ambassador and how mamaliga, an Eastern European bread, played such a huge role in their food culture that it connected them at a state dinner.

Just so you know, mamaliga (mama-leegah) is the Moldovan equivalent of cornbread—a much wetter cornbread. Mamaliga (besides being a fun word to say) was a traditional peasant dish of Moldova and Romania but is now very common and available in even high-end traditional restaurants. (It's somewhat similar to Italian polenta.) Mamaliga is made by boiling water, salt, and cornmeal in a shallow cast-iron pot with a curved bottom. It can be made two ways: thicker, where it can be cut into slices like bread, or softer, similar to the consistency of thick oatmeal.

Since mamaliga is sticky and will stick to a knife when fresh, it is often cut with a sewing thread. Typically, this dish is served with shaved brinza (salty, homemade cheese) and meat or fish, but sometimes there's sour cream or garlic on the side, or it's crushed into a bowl of hot milk. It's the perfect combination of hearty, salty, and tasty, if done right and, most importantly, eaten fresh. If you want to taste Moldova, order fried fish, brinza, sour cream, garlic, and mamaliga; it's a unique combination of tastes and textures unlike anything else." [7]

He described mamaliga as a more solid polenta, but in Moldova it's like bread. He said, "back in history, our great grandfathers and grandmothers, they probably used mamaliga as a sort of polenta that was a replacement for bread. They also prepared mamaliga because they said that it much healthier than bread oftentimes. I thought this was something that we only ate in Moldova until I discovered that Italians used

7   Leah Kieff, "Foods You Must Try In Moldova," Peacecorps.gov, December 10, 2015.

to eat mamaliga long ago." He shared that he found that they used different ingredients and that the textures were different. He hinted that this may have come from the times when those countries used to be part of the Roman Empire and shared various recipes.

Veaceslav gave me a brief but essential history lesson, saying that there was a lot of tension within the Roman Empire and there were many conflicts that resulted from that. However, the beauty that lies within that conflict was the influence of language, tradition, and food. He said that, "the Roman Empire contained countries like Romania, Moldova, Ukraine, Belgium, Italy, Spain, France, and many other countries. There's everlasting roots of Latin through the Romanian language, like the old Romance languages, French, Portuguese, Spanish, Romanian language, so to speak, also going back to keep it out if it's related to the language, but it is similar to the foods that we eat like the form of polenta. Polenta being what it's known to be in some parts of Europe, and it being known as mamaliga in Moldova."

He also shared that hospitality and food culture throughout Eastern Europe is almost the same because "traditionally, in most Eastern European countries, you will find that the first thing that someone will do after meeting you is invite you into their home. To get closer and to establish mutual trust, they will share their food and possibly share recipes and exchange recipes or preparation customs with you. They use this opportunity to condense the awkward silent moments of a conversation and try to build a relationship between the persons. This as an important part of the culture, in the country.

This conversation with Veaceslav reminded me of my recent interview with my colleague Nadia from the National Geographic Channel. She shared with me how food is the catalyst of formulating relationships and bonds. For when she travels for personal reasons and visits her family in India, she often meets cousins or distant family members that she had not been in constant communication with. However, they would invite her into their home and have appetizers or a dish and the laughs and conversation followed.

Luciano Pavarotti was right when he said, "one of the very nicest things about life is the way we must regularly stop whatever it is we are doing and devote our attention to eating."[8] Throughout all of these stories and experiences, I have come to believe that we were created to have some sort of connection, understanding, and exchange with one another, and food has found its way to mend everything together. In a way food leaves it imprints in our memories and finds its way into our DNA, and we begin to find that we often identify with our cultures through food. In a future chapter, I'll discuss how food culture plays a role in how we engage with one another and how we share our identities through our cuisines.

---

8   Luciano Pavarotti, "Luciano Pavarotti Quotable Quote," Goodreads.com, 2020.

2

CUISINES AND CULTURAL IDENTITY

———

FOOD AND TRAVEL

When you're planning for a trip, do you research which restaurants, coffee shops, pastry stops, or food trucks you're going to visit? Well, according to the World Food Travel Association, since 2018, "Food has finally become a main motivation for travelers when choosing a destination. Travelers began to spend more time and money on unique food and beverage experiences. We saw a global increase in the number of food tour companies, food-and-beverage focused events, and food-and-beverage-experience focused marketing efforts. Food tourism is finally mainstream."[9]

Food tourism is defined as "The pursuit and enjoyment of unique and memorable food and drink experiences, both far

———

9   "Evolution of Food Tourism," World Food Tourism, 2020.

and near."[10] As of late, I have been reading about culinary tourism, watching food tourist shows, following multiple food pages on Instagram, and pinning multiple appetizer boards on Pinterest because I enjoy trying and making new foods. Oftentimes, I find myself also wanting to learn different recipes in the different countries or states I've visited. I've traveled to the Bahamas (Little San Salvador Island and Freeport), Haiti (Port-au Prince, Cap Haitian, Jacmel, Hinche, Les Cayes, Petition-Ville, and Delmas), Dominican Republic, Vietnam (Ho Chi Minh City and Mekong Delta), South Korea (Seoul), China (Beijing and Hong Kong), the United Kingdom (London and Bath) and fifteen of the states within the United States. What I remember most in all of these trips was the cultural connections through conversation and food.

So, I began to wonder what motivates people to travel and what I have found is that everyone loves traveling, for there's sightseeing, meeting new people, and, in my case, making new friends; the ability to take Segway or Hop-on-Hop-off tours; and the endless amounts of Instagram posts that we create to make our friends and family jealous.

But the best part of it all is the food and here are the top ten reasons why:

- Challenging **yourself to something new**
- Learning
- Expanding your **perspective**
- Practicing self-care

---

10   Erik Wolf, "Culinary Tourism: A Tasty Economic Proposition," World Food Tourism, 2001.

- Getting in touch with yourself
- Building and strengthening **relationships**
- Having an **adventure**
- Escaping
- Celebrating
- Relaxing and rejuvenating

Out of these ten, there are four points that I want to focus on throughout this chapter: ***challenging yourself to something new, expanding your perspective, building and strengthening relationships, and relaxing and rejuvenating.*** While the reasoning behind why people travel may be for all four of these points and more, it plays a role in our cultural identities and understanding of other culture groups.

CULTURE IDENTITIES AND CULTURE GROUPS

What I have found is that everyone loves traveling regardless if it is national or international, for there is sightseeing, meeting new people, and, in my case, making new friends; the ability to go on excursions; and the endless amounts of Instagram posts that we create to make our friends and family jealous. But the best part of it all is the food. I read a Spoon University article and can completely agree with their statement that "Different areas of the world have so many new flavors and dishes that you would never even think of. From decadent scoops of gelato to exotic acarajé, there is always something fun to try. The possibilities are endless."[11]

---

11   Siobhan Miller et al., "5 Reasons Eating Will Always Be the Best Part About Traveling," *Her Campus Media LLC,* 2019.

One of the four points of why people travel that I want to focus on is *challenging yourself*. The US is a called melting pot; however, if you think about it, it really is not because everything doesn't look the same and every region has something to offer. I love Californian tacos with fries, Kansas City BBQ, New York's deli bacon egg and cheese on a croissant, DC's Mumbo sauce on fried chicken, Nashville hot chicken, Cajun alligator tail, and the list goes on.

Moreover, when you take the leap of faith and travel beyond our borders, you find so many dishes in other countries that you would never try if you did not challenge yourself or be curious enough to travel there. Traveling somewhere new opens your eyes and your taste buds to a whole new range of authentic flavor profiles and foods that you would have otherwise been missing out on.

In terms of *perspective*, if you've traveled to Poland, you know about the famous pierogis, a traditional Polish dumpling stuffed with various meats and vegetables. I had similar experiences in Vietnam; I love banh mi and boba tea and would only spend maybe three US dollars for a 12-inch sandwich and a boba tea with toppings. I also enjoyed all the various pho dishes and ways to egg-based appetizers and dishes. Moreover, while in Vietnam I became obsessed with the French influence within Vietnamese cuisine.

For example, choux à la crème (cream puffs) is called bánh su kem in Vietnamese. This pastry is French inspired but has been vamped by Vietnamese flavors and culture. During a global residency trip, my Vietnamese study buddies, Wendy, Nhi, Khanh, and Tân, took me and my roommate, Sanasa, to a pastry shop where they sold bành su kem by the dozen; some were jelly-filled and others had chocolate drizzle with custard in between. It immediately won my heart. Look at that beauty. Wouldn't you appreciate enjoying this bite in Vietnam as well? Without getting into why Vietnam was a French colony, I seem to sometimes find the beauty within gory pasts, and that includes influence in food and culture. This is also some of the beauties of food fusion. This brought on a cultural conversation amongst me, Sanasa, Wendy, Nhi, Khanh, and Tân about food fusion. Being that I had some French influence within my Haitian culture, Sanasa had some French influence within her Guinean culture, and Vietnamese has some French influence in its culture, this very conversation about food and fusion was able to bridge the gaps of our various cultures and *form friendship*.

I recently read an article that shared some other French influence within Vietnamese cuisine, like onions. As you may or may not know, onions are one of the backbones of French cuisine. In Vietnam, they are known as hành tay, and they're often quick-pickled and used as a garnish for other dishes like pho. *Side note: When ordering Pho, if you want to add some more flavor to your soup, ask for Hanh Dam, Vietnamese-style pickled onions in vinegar. I promise you'll thank me later.*

Now back to French influence in Vietnamese cuisine:

Coffee is yet another ingredient you'll find more commonly in Vietnam than in surrounding areas. The French had started drinking coffee in the 1600s when it was introduced from the Middle East and brought it with them to Vietnam 200 years later. It was quickly adapted into the local cuisine and culture, largely because Vietnam has an excellent climate for growing coffee—the proof: today, Vietnam is the world's second largest coffee exporter. As opposed to

French coffee, which is usually served hot and black as espresso or with steamed milk as café au lait, Vietnamese coffee is usually drunk cold and sweetened with condensed milk. But coffee is also a great example of how the locals in Vietnam absorbed the French influence. It wasn't in accepting it as-is, but rather in integrating these new additions in their own way, tailoring the ingredients to their way of eating and cooking.[12]

The same goes for bread:

Bread is not common in East Asia, but when the French colonists arrived in Vietnam, you can bet they came armed with baguettes. The Vietnamese adapted this bread and began using it in their local cuisine; you can find Vietnamese baguettes even today on

12   Emily Monaco, "The French Influence on Vietnamese Cuisine," *Epicure & Culture*, 2015.

pretty much every corner. The other main difference between the two baguettes is in the style of the bread itself; while the Vietnamese style of baguette is similar to the French baguette, it is made with rice flour instead of wheat flour, giving it a wholly distinct flavor and texture. These baguettes are used as the base of one of the most famous Vietnamese dishes worldwide, banh mi. The sandwiches contain a combination of grilled meat, coriander, pickled vegetables and pâté, a true amalgam of the Vietnamese penchant for fresh herbs and crisp, raw vegetables and the French influences of pâté and meat.[13]

What I've learned is that by discovering a new food or bite while traveling is enough reason to go back to a country someday and while **relaxing and rejuvenating**, you can enjoy

---

13   Ibid.

it again with friends that you made. So, if you've traveled a lot, you have a lot of countries to visit in the near future or you have the opportunity to recreate certain dishes.

While discovering completely new foods in a foreign country is amazing, so is trying a food you've eaten many times before and finding a completely new flavor in it. Foods in other countries have so much more flavor than the American versions of them. For example, calzones in Italy has so much more flavor than the hot pockets at your nearest grocery store. The taste and texture can be so different that it may seem like you are trying a new food for the first time.14

Siobhan Miller and Ashley Peek from Spoon University outlined five reasons why food will always be the best part of traveling. Of these five reasons, I want to focus on four: *learning about a country's culture through their food, experiencing foods you eat at home in a new way, food bringing people together, and gaining new flavors and dishes to try at home.*

"Tell me what you eat, and I will tell you who you are."
—*JEAN ANTHELME BRILLAT-SAVARIN*[15]

---

14 Siobhan Miller et al., 5 Reasons Eating Will Always Be the Best Part About Traveling, *Her Campus Media LLC*, 2019.

15 Jean Anthelme Brillat-Savarin, BrainyQuote.com, *BrainyMedia*, Inc. 2020.

FOOD CULTURE

A country's food tells you a lot about their culture. The term *food culture* "refers to the practices, attitudes, and beliefs as well as the networks and institutions surrounding the production, distribution, and consumption of food."[16] As I shared about Vietnam and the various dishes that contain French influence, it's so cool to travel to a different country and experience a portion of their culture and what they value based on their food and dining styles. Take Costa Rica for example. "The country's motto is *pura vida* which means 'pure life.' The country and its people truly embody that. Their staple meal is a meal consisting of rice, sweet plantains, and your choice of either beef, chicken, or fish, all of which are very fresh. It's such a simple meal because that's what they as a country and culture represent: simplicity. Therefore, you can expect a lot of fresh fish and chicken, a lot of beautiful fresh fruit, and rice."[17] Part of this simplicity in Costa Rican food culture is taken in while having a great time sharing a meal with family and friends.

If you look at French food culture, according to UNESCO, it is important for them to be "bringing people together to enjoy the art of good eating and drinking and the power to create togetherness, the pleasure of taste, and the balance between human beings and the products of nature."[18] "Their

---

16 Megan Faletra, "What Is Food Culture and How Does It Impact Health?" *The Well Essentials,* 2020.

17 Siobhan Miller et al., 5 Reasons Eating Will Always Be the Best Part About Traveling, *Her Campus Media LLC,* 2019.

18 Dominique Cachat, "A Guide to French Cuisine," Expatica, September 14, 2020.

staple foods are [artisan breads], fine cuts of meat, decadent desserts, expensive cheese, and beautiful wine (often the two are paired together). "They as a country tend to value the finer things in life—for them, it's better to eat a small amount of something truly exquisite than a lot of a poorer-quality product. The Parisian aesthetic is elegance and class at every turn."[19]

Travel also allows you experience to foods you eat at home in a new way. In my own experience, I found the English cream tea blowing my mind of understanding how to enjoy an afternoon teatime with tea, English scones (a.k.a. biscuits), clotted cream, and jam. I'm from the South, so going into this I had my bias of what good homemade biscuits (scones) were to taste like. However, once I tried cream tea, my perspective changed. I now oftentimes crave the clotted cream and jam portion over a good homemade biscuit. If I didn't get the opportunity to study Jane Austen and other major women writers, I don't think I would have gotten the chance to travel to London during that time and partake in trying cream tea. So, travel does indeed allow one to experience the foods that you are accustomed to in a new way.

Food brings people together. I know you're probably saying to yourself, "Kathiana, doesn't this need its own chapter?" I've already thought ahead, and the answer is yes—chapter 5. However, I wanted to briefly connect the dots of people becoming closer with one another through food and travel.

---

19   Siobhan Miller et al., 5 Reasons Eating Will Always Be the Best Part About Traveling, *Her Campus Media LLC*, 2019.

There's nothing better than experiencing new food with others who are just as ecstatic about it as you are. Find a family member or a friend that shares the same love of food that you may have. You'll bond over the amazing new foods you try, what you should try next, and what cool restaurants you should go to while traveling. Food also helps you meet new people. It is always cool to strike up a conversation with a stranger at the table over about their dessert that looks just as good as the picture on the menu. You may make a new friend and try something new that you may never have thought to try.[20]

To travel is to eat; therefore, you gain new flavors and dishes to try at home. "Going to a new country and trying new dishes and experiencing new flavors means you get to come home with so many things to try in your own kitchen. Sure, it might not taste exactly like that pasta you had in Rome, but hey in the real world you can tell yourself it's just as good, right? One of the best parts of traveling and trying new things is to bring home that knowledge you didn't have before, so take advantage of it. The kitchen is a place where you can travel to any country without having to ever leave your house, so get cooking, friends."[21]

Last year I started my own Instagram food page in hopes of sharing recipes that have been passed down to me in my family or inspirations from my travels. Moreover, due to COVID-19, I have found myself recreating meals like bulgogi, chicken

---

20 Ibid.

21 Ibid.

alfredo, pizzas, brunch casseroles, hibachi bowls, smoothie bowls, and desserts to mentally take me back to a time when I was able to travel. However, when I first started my page, my goal was to share recipes that have either Haitian or Southern Soul Food influence. We all have this desire to share our meals with others to build our social connections. Part of that desire is to share our culture with someone to bring light to our background and memories.

WHAT IS CULTURE IDENTITY?

The formal meaning of culture identity is:

> . . . the shared characteristics of a group of people, which encompasses, place of birth, religion, language, cuisine, social behaviors, art, literature, and music. Some cultures are widespread and have a large number of people who associate themselves with those particular values, beliefs, and origins. Others are relatively small, with only a small number of people who associate themselves with that culture. However, the value of culture cannot be defined by its size. No matter if a culture is widespread or kept within a small region, is young or old, or has changed over time or stayed the same, every culture can teach us about ourselves, others, and the global community.
>
> Cultural identity is constructed and maintained through the process of sharing collective knowledge such as traditions, heritage, language, aesthetics, norms and customs. As individuals typically affiliate

with more than one cultural group, cultural identity is complex and multifaceted.[22]

I personally identify myself as Haitian American. My family became citizens of the United States back in the 1980s and I was born in Atlanta, GA. So, I get the pleasantries of both Southern Soul food and Caribbean. I love being Haitian American mostly because of the food and, of course, the culture. When I think of the dishes that would be prepared in my family, I oftentimes think of the *diri kole ak pwa, poule nan sos, banan peze, pikliz, fritay, macaroni gratine, salade russe, jus grenadia, ou jus mango.* However, if I were to go to my Auntie Barbara, Alma, or Janice's house, I can expect to be enjoying *fried chicken, smothered turkey wings, mac and cheese, collard greens, fried corn, squash casserole, green beans, baked salmon, okra, black-eyed peas, banana pudding, peach cobbler, Kool-Aid, lemonade,* or sweet tea. The beauty about these two cultures is not only the preparation, but also something that I hold deep within me and would be able to relate with a fellow Haitian or African American individual. These meals are something that I would share because I am proud of who I am and would like others to enjoy or feast in meals that are served in my culture.

After talking to a few friends, I found that they related to having their own cultural identities and wanting to share that with others.

---

22 Vivian Hsueh-Hua Chen, "Cultural Identity," *Key Concepts in Intercultural Dialogue* 22, no. 1 (2014).

MANAL'S STORY

Like my friend Manal, whom I met at National Geographic. She told me about her experience of moving from Pakistan to attend the University of California, Berkeley at twenty-two years old. Fortunately, she'd had the opportunity to travel during her youth, but what I found interesting in our conversation was when she said that "the first time that you move away from home it's a complicated time and you get a lot of complex feelings." While she was excited to take on the world and wanted to meet new people, learn, grow, and soak in a great experience at one of the top universities in the States, she would find herself during the first couple of weeks trying to find Pakistani food or restaurants close to campus. And luckily there were quite a few of them because Indian and Pakistani food is very popular. Often when she would plan to go out to eat, she would go to those restaurants because she felt that she and other students from abroad or immigrants would make these places focal points of the community. For that's where you go and you eat, and it's basically the food that brings people together and reminds them of home.

She continued to say that like "most cultures, the Pakistani culture is very big, very big on food, and it's a very family-oriented culture." So, her family would always like sit down around the table for meals. "Like my dad made it a point to do that; that wasn't the case in every family, but for him that was really important that we were all sitting there without the gadgets." (I grew up in a different time.) So, they would gather around the table for breakfast, lunch, and dinner and that was just a ritual they would enjoy together and that would also be the time to catch up about the day. Manal said that those moments when she has dinner around the table with friends now draws her back to those moments with her family.

She also finds that sitting around the table to enjoy a meal is still very important to her. She also shares her experience of the ambiance of the restaurants where she would eat:

> *In terms of food I mean, [. . .] from the time that I moved to Berkeley, I've been basically [living] abroad, you know, most of the time in between then and now all my way back home, out of here in the middle, but I've been either in the States, and then later I moved to New York, and later, when I moved to Spain, so I even there. I mean, it was always like okay where's the, you know, find the nearest Pakistani or Indian restaurants because it was just, it's not just even the food. Like, you walk in there, your music, you hear the waiters talking your language. You can have like, especially you know, you have a connection and then when you open the menu, you see like all these things in your familiar language. . . . If you would take your American [friends] there for example, you would have this, like. sense of pride and being able to, like, own the menu and say , "Oh no, I'm gonna take care of it, you know."*

She'd feel like those restaurants were her domain because this is what she'd grown up with, and so it was not something that she would do consciously, just what kind of happened that she would feel this pride in taking foreign or American friends. They're speaking to the waiters and ordering but not in her precious native language, but she is able to read the menu and say all the words the way they're supposed to be said, you know; there's little things like that.

And I think that kind of speaks to just a larger cultural identity, but here in the US, we're obviously very multicultural. It's very much a multicultural country, but then the places where we are able to taste that culture literally are our restaurants. There aren't many communities, I mean there's community centers for different cultures, but people who are not part of the community wouldn't go there. So, what the restaurant comes to symbolize is much bigger than just food. It's really like a pizza place where you feel, you know, a culture that's not yours and is yours. But you are kind of away from it, so you want to reconnect with it.

Like Manal, one of my friends, Jane Zimmerman who is a former US ambassador, shared with me her experience with culture identity, but through the Greeks and the Turks.

GREEKS AND THE TURKS

I'll even tell you like, for instance, I told you how, like the Greek Cypriots [and] the Turkish Cypriots would argue over everything. So one of the things they [Greeks] particularly criticized, you know, is American policy because they feel the US takes more the pro-Turkish line, and they think we should just go ahead and march the Turkish military off anyway. But one of the things I found was that they kept talking about these issues, and sometimes I just [saw] it was a circular discussion. We were just getting nowhere, and so one of the things I discovered was that the only thing [they could] talk about was potatoes.

For some reason, they all agreed on the potatoes, not the tomato, potato. Reason being is that they are rightfully proud of their potato. And I found that when I wanted to make them stop talking about the politics of things, I would just bring up potatoes. For example, I would say, inevitably, at any meeting, if you put up a fight and I find a way to work with the conversation and just say, you know, there's no potato like a Cypress potato, and then [the conversation] will go completely to the subject of their potatoes and how wonderful they were, and we could get a break. And I mentioned this one time to the British ambassador, high commissioner. And I was at the dinner display. And he was having something like a rice and curry. And we were having the same conversation with a bunch of friends like we'd been having every day. We were getting nowhere with it, right. I look up and go, oh you know, "Peter, Mr. Ambassador, this rice and curry is delicious. But you know, there's no potato like a Cypress potato." It was good. . . . And sure enough, everybody else went on talking about their potatoes. We would eventually get work done but to catch a break, Cypress potatoes would often be my saving grace.

It's incredible to think that something as simple a potato is able to bridge a connection between two cultures and calm the air. Essentially, we were created to have some sort of connection, understanding, and exchange with one another. While I was able to create a friendship out of my food fusion conversations in Vietnam, I find it so interesting how our desire to share our cultural identities through food brings a sense of understanding and peace. Whether it's traveling that brings light to our interest or shift in perspective of another culture, or our desire to educate others about our own cultures, there is a connection that is formed between our love for a culture, or likes or love for others during our palate's experiences.

3

MEALS AND MEMORY

There is power in our palates. Kathiana, what do you mean by that? First, let's define both the words power and palate.

According to Vocabulary.com, "*Power* comes from the Latin word *potere*, which means "to be able."[23] But things with power are much more than able; they're able to exert a lot of force. "The powers that be" are those who hold authority, and "the power behind the throne" refers to the people who exert influence without being formally in charge . . . possession of controlling influence."[24] Now, the meaning of the word power that we will use is to be able to influence.

On the other hand, your *palate* means your taste. It's also defined as "a person's appreciation of taste and flavor, especially when sophisticated and discriminating."[25] (Also, when you touch your tongue to the top of your mouth, what you're

---

23   *Vocabulary.com*, s.v. "power (n.)," accessed March 12, 2020.

24   Ibid.

25   *Oxford Dictionary* on Lexico, s.v. "palate (n.)," Lexico Dictionaries English, accessed March 12, 2020.

touching is your palate.) Palate is often used when discussing taste in a broader sense, as in "Eating chocolate chip pancakes is pleasing to the palate of some people."

Both your palate and internal power plays hand in hand when deciding what you enjoy eating versus what you don't enjoy eating. I use the two words power and palate together because, when you try a dish for the first time from another culture, your palate has the power to determine if your taste buds enjoyed it or not. For, as we age our palate also seems to develop and everyone starts enjoying a few things that they did not as a child. For example, I used to hate Brussels sprouts and now I can't live without them. The same goes for asparagus; if anything I have found that if I add garlic confit to my asparagus, I can enjoy it with a side of baked sweet potatoes and grilled chicken, versus having broccoli as an option for greens. This same power that allows you to now enjoy dishes that you probably wouldn't have in the past helps you in telling others to try it.

YOUR PALATE

I wanted to discuss the paradigm of authority versus power, and how that works. Throughout my writing process, I have been asking people what the words power and authority mean to them. And some people would just say well, authority has a negative connotation to it and I don't like that word, or power has a negative connotation to it and I don't like that word, but our palates, our taste buds, or the meaning of palate is to allow us to decide what we like and what we don't like and to form our perspective of it. And it's the power within ourselves that allows us to engage the different food flavors or cuisines that become our palate, and it's so powerful that it can help us break the ice of understanding another culture or another group of people. For example, any kid can be a picky eater but as their palate develops, they try new things. For new moms, being pregnant changes their palates change just as their perspective changes.

So, it's interesting to see all those things work together and how they can inform diplomacy, but I feel like power and palate can help drive the conversation. The whole point of diplomacy, from a political standpoint, is to help manage the international relationships of your country and to explain what your culture stands for or believes in. I feel like that's a sense of cultural identity as well because you wouldn't allow yourself to pledge allegiance to a country and go manage, defend, or speak on issues that are important and valuable to you if you didn't feel a part of the culture. I feel like it's the same with food.

According to a colleague of mine, every culture has a form of dumpling. They could be like biscuits, they could be empanadas or patties, or they could be your Asian dumplings that are either fried or boiled, but every culture has this form of comfort in a ball. In the same way, our palate's power and perception traces back to our home or experiences. Have you ever had a dish with a story that was passed on from generation to generation in your family? Maybe it includes key ingredients that have been kept sacred and you dare not share what the secret ingredient is? If so, you can agree that when you share or serve this dish to entertain or to potluck with friends, there is a joy in sharing the dish and being proud of the story behind the dish or how it's been passed on to you.

SOUP JOUMOU

For example, every year each Haitian family brings in the New Year by celebrating not only the new year, but also by celebrating the joys of our Independence Day. We do this by not only dancing and cheering, but by also enjoying a large bowl of pumpkin soup, formally called Soup Joumou.

Kelly Paulemon, a Haitian travel writer wrote an amazing article that shares a brief history of the Soup. "Soup Joumou is a delicious and aromatic dish with a dense history, dating back to the French occupation of Haiti, dating back to when it was a favorite of French slave owners in eighteenth-century Haiti."[26]

"*Joumou* is the Kreyòl word derived from *giraumon* in French, which means 'pumpkin' in English. If you're an avid fall cook,

26 Kelly Paulemon, "Soup Joumou—the Taste of Freedom," *Visit Haiti*, December 2018.

you might see joumou-varietal pumpkins at some specialty supermarkets in the United States. They're easy to spot at Haiti's sprawling farmers markets."[27]

The soup is traditionally based on a large winter squash that resembles a pumpkin, but it's packed with other ingredients and flavor. Here's how you would make it:

INGREDIENTS:
- Butternut squash
- Meat option (turkey, chicken, or beef)
- Cow's foot (optional)
- Potatoes
- Parsley
- Carrots
- Green cabbage
- Celery
- Plantains (optional)
- Epis (blend of herbs and spices)
- Thin pasta (vermicelli or spaghetti)
- Macaroni shells
- Vinegar
- Lime
- Salt
- Pepper
- Garlic
- Green onion
- Bell pepper (your preference)
- Scotch bonnet pepper

---

27   Ibid.

- Olive oil
- Thyme

PREP PROCESS:

The butternut squash is skinned and cut into slices. The other vegetables are then peeled and diced (potatoes, carrots, cabbage, and celery).

Make your epis complete: Blend parsley, green onion, garlic, bell pepper, black pepper, and olive oil or other cooking oil.

Clean and season your meat options and cow's foot (optional) with vinegar and lime, and then add your epis.

COOKING PROCESS:

The slices of the squash are then boiled in a pot.

(If you decide to make it with a cow's foot, pressure-cook it on the side with water close to the rim for about an hour or an hour and a half on medium heat.)

Then cook your meat option as desired.

Puree butternut squash and preserve the puree in another bowl or keep it in the blender until you're ready for the next step.

In a bigger pot, add cooking oil with carrots, potatoes, plantains, and thyme; once browned add celery and add butternut squash puree with about one to two more cups of water, salt, and scotch bonnet pepper. Once this boils, add the pasta with meat and green cabbage and cook it into deliciousness.

Feel free to sample and add more spices as desired. Once soup is ready serve it hot. It is usually accompanied with a sliced Haitian bread and either ginger tea or hot chocolate as a beverage.

* * *

STORY BEHIND THE SOUP

Haitian families enjoy the soup because it is known to be the taste of liberty and freedom. Here's a brief history lesson about the soup:

> *In 19th-century Haiti, living conditions for slaves were unspeakably awful. As elsewhere in the world, they were treated brutally, kept enslaved by a combination of gruesome physical treatment and psychological abuse. Slave masters denied these people as much as possible, even seemingly trivial things, especially if those things were associated with the lifestyle of Haiti's French slave-owning bourgeoise. One tradition that was well established within the bourgeoisie was that of having soup joumou. Some households could afford to make it several times a week, others only on Sundays, but a bowl of soup joumou was never to be seen in the hands or mouths of a slave. This food was not intended for them, as it was too rich, too wholesome, too good . . . . Therefore, in the first years of the*

19th century, slaves and free black Haitians led a successful revolution, taking control of the country and instating their own language, their own institutions, and their own customs. As a potent symbol of the abundance that had been denied them for hundreds of years, the newly free population appropriated the food most symbolic of freedom: soup joumou. Independence was officially declared on January 1st, 1804. To celebrate that first New Year's Day, the people of Haiti prepared, cooked, and shared soup joumou. A delicacy previously forbidden, it was now made available to everyone. More than two hundred years later, the tradition is still going strong.[28]

Growing up, I never really liked the soup unless there would only be chicken, noodles, carrots, and celery in my bowl. For the dish has several veggies within it, and what kid likes vegetables, not this one. However, the older I got the more I enjoyed the other ingredients within the soup, and I have taken pride of what the soup is and the history that it holds. Moreover, I find that me and my cousins obsess over the soup and try to tell our friends to come over and partake in the goodness of the soup. Now, looking back I have noticed the power in means of influence that the bowl of soup holds: It holds part of my history, culture, past-times fun, tasty bites, and memories.

I know that many other cultures can relate to having a specific dish, just like soup joumou, that has a story and was passed down from generation to generation, and you can

---

28   Ibid.

probably relate to the power that the dish holds in your family. Maybe oftentimes you, too, rave to your friends how they must try the dish and also experience the goodness in the flavor that it contains along with the story that is associated with it. Somehow, when our friends do finally get a taste of the dish we refer to, there is a sense of connection that happens, especially if they enjoy it.

As I mentioned in a previous chapter, food is a catalyst that brings individuals together. To add to that point, our palates in a way bring us closer because of either the appreciation or rejection of a particular flavor. For example, I remember there would be times that I was eating either my mom's or one of my auntie's rice and beans, and I would mistake a bean for a whole clove, yuck. While I would enjoy eating the rice and beans, the cloves would automatically ruin my taste buds. Fortunately, in recent years, my family members have converted to using clove powder, so my younger cousins have been spared from that experience. When I meet with other Haitian American youth, one of many things that brings us together is someone bringing up how they don't enjoy cloves, also known as *jirof*.

One other dish that I can't seem to escape and that I embrace as a part of my culture is *diri kole ak pwa*, also known as Haitian rice and beans. This is a side or sometimes entree option that you will find in every Haitian, Creole, or Latin household. The difference between Haitian rice and beans and that of other groups is that Haitian rice and beans are mixed in together; it's not exactly what you think. My favorite rice and bean option is cranberry beans and rice. Here's what you would need:

INGREDIENTS:

- Cranberry beans
- Rice
- Epis (blended spices)
- Cloves of garlic, minced
- Stems of thyme
- Scotch bonnet pepper (optional)
- Clove powder
- Water
- Salt
- Coconut milk (optional)
- Oil

INSTRUCTIONS:

First you boil your beans. Be sure to use enough water so that it cooks the beans and add more water along the way so that it does not boil away.

Once your beans are cooked, you drain them and reserve the liquid for later

You then take a pot and add oil and epis (herbs and season mix) and once it's browned, add your beans and thyme with a dash of clove powder and salt. After stirring the pot, add the reserved bean liquid. Once that boils, add your rice. Once the rice water reduces, add the coconut milk. Let rice simmer, and then voila: You have your rice and beans!

UNIVERSAL STYLES OF RICE

It amazes me how rice and beans or rice dishes can vary based on where you are in the world. It's also fascinating how these rice recipes serve as a memory that often tie us to our cultural identity. I recently watched a Tasty video on Facebook called Party Rice around Africa. It showed off various rice recipes, like Kenyan Beef and Potato Pilau, Ghanaian Jollof rice, Somali Bariis, and Cape Verde Arroz de Marisco. In the video, I remember that each person who cooked and showed off their dish would explain a popular event or time that they would enjoy these rice dishes.

For example, for the Kenyan beef and potato pilau, the person cooking it, Kiano Moju, Tasty team representative, mentioned that you would find these at the best parties and how cooking is a part of the party. Kiano also added how the best pilau has beef and potatoes. When Tei Hammond, another Tasty team representative, was cooking the Ghanaian Jollof rice, he mentioned that depending on who is making the rice, it can be spicy but still something that they enjoy as a family. Amal Dalmar, another Tasty team member, who was making Somali bariis, also adds that in her culture, bariis is easy to make but how everyone makes it is different. She also went on to say that while bariis is often served at some parties, the main event that they would serve bariis is at weddings. One of the cool things I noticed that they add to their rice is fried onions and orange-dyed French fries. When the video got to Kiki Canuto, to cook the Cape Verde arroz de marisco, she explained how to make it and said how it's a party in your mouth and how in her culture, they constantly dance and party and are surrounded by family and friends to have a good time. Kiki's part of the video reminded me of paella and how me and my friends would have a good time while also enjoying food.

While each culture dresses rice different, I think we can all relate to having memories around sharing that meal. The reason that I mentioned this video is that while they only focused on various African rice dishes, they expressed their palate and how these dishes tied to a memory and their culture identity and wanted to share that with the world. Think about your own family or friend dynamics and parties you've been to, while food wasn't the ultimate center of the event, it is still something that you remember to be either really good or really bad. Moreover, those memories and meal exchanges are something that has a deeper connection than we understand.

RESEARCH ON FOOD AND MEMORY

I've always been amazed of how food and memory our connected. Years ago, I came across a book written by anthropologist and author John Allen, titled *The Omnivorous Mind: Our Evolving Relationship with Food*. He said, "We all have our food memories, some good and some bad. The taste, smell, and texture of food can be extraordinarily evocative, bringing back memories not just of eating food itself but also of place and setting. Food is an effective trigger of deeper memories of feelings and emotions, internal states of the mind and body."[29] All of our senses are powerful; however, I want to shed emphasis on how powerful our palate is and

---

29   John Allen, *The Omnivorous Mind: Our Evolving Relationship with Food*, (United States: Harvard University Press, 2012).

how it is influenced by our ability to smell. The combination of smell and taste is quite literally what memories are made of. Oftentimes, when I reflect on certain memories throughout my life, most of them include food in some way or another.

For example, my grandmother passed away in September of 2019, and one of the many things that cheers me up is remembering the times that she would have me and my sisters and cousins in the making or preparing of dishes for Sunday dinner, or watching her make some of the best fish and grits and getting to sample everything, every step of the way. Other memories that come to mind when I think of the times that we spent in our family kitchen was making a Haitian alcoholic beverage called *cremas* and handing over all the ingredients and watching her or my mom stir the mixture, strain it, and bottle it. Then we'd often gift it to family friends for Christmas or their birthdays. Like me, you can probably reminisce on those times either in the kitchen, on the grill, or eating and enjoying a meal with a family or friend.

When I set back and think of my travel memories, I often gaze and reminisce over images of not only gorgeous landscapes, skyscrapers, or quaint towns or villages, but also of dinners, unforgettable pastries, teas, best coffee and topping combinations, or unique and playful main courses. And in the reverse, I can take a bite of something and immediately go back to wherever I was when I first tried that flavor or dish. I have come to realize that while food is not the absolute reason that I hold on to or have those memories, it plays a big role; the experience or exchange amplified those memories. The experiences and exchanges that were created while enjoying the food are almost always unforgettable. All of the times spent with family learning new skills, celebrating life's moments, having a good time allows those memories to last forever. The physical act of enjoying the food itself most likely lasts only minutes, but the memory linked to that food experience can last a lifetime. With the holidays being around the corner, I look forward to the process of creating amazing dishes and new memories that will be made around the table.

HOSPITALITY AND CULTURAL IDENTITY

I was talking to my colleague, Nadia about culture identity and how we can identify with our cultures sometimes because of food, and she shared an interesting perspective. Nadia has traveled to Mexico, Canada, the United Kingdom, Amsterdam, Spain, France, Morocco, Kenya, Turkey, Dubai, Oman, Saudi Arabia, India, Singapore, Hong Kong, and several states within the United States. Throughout her travels and dining experiences, she has found that most cultures, if not all cultures, show hospitality through food. So, forming personal or business connections with different people around the world has often been over food or drinks. People want to talk about their culture and tell you more about their lives over food, not necessarily wanting to talk about the food. While you can ask questions about the food, that isn't the main topic of discussion. Because when you sit down, they tell you things about their daily lives, their worldviews, or whatever else it may be, but in the end, they always want you to enjoy your food.

For example, while I once thought the South of the United States, West Indian islands and most Asian countries that I've traveled to in the past were hospitable, or that Middle Eastern dining experiences to be very hospitable and tasty, I've never considered or thought of the Eurasian Caucasus country of Georgia, until one of my colleagues, Amy, mentioned an article National Geographic wrote on things to know before enjoying your Georgian feast.

The article touches on the traditional Georgian feast known as supra, and how it is prepared. At supra, the dishes would be laid out family-style on the table, and all of the dishes were made from scratch. (Dishes made from scratch hold a special place in my heart because that means there was some love added to it and you can always "taste" that.) During the supra, there's also a toastmaster and you normally follow their lead. The feast can go one for hours with wine, dancing, and eating, for there's always more than enough food. They eat and entertain this way because hospitality means a lot to them. After reading the article and reflecting on my travel experiences, I can agree with Nadia's point that food is a catalyst for other opportunities in means of a connection, memory, or good times.

FOOD, MEMORY, AND HOSPITALITY

These dishes and memories connect to our cultural identity and always brings us back to something that reminds us of home. For example, I'll never forget meeting some of my friends at Marymount University. Something that drew me close with this group was talking about my cousin Mimi's mac and cheese, and my mom and aunts making Haitian food. Some upperclassmen heard my chatter with my group of friends and invited us to the Soul Food night event on campus. At this Soul Food dinner, they gave a brief history of why in Black communities we prepare certain dishes, and it blew my mind. They also talked about how things are made based on region and why certain Soul Food dishes have certain flavor depending on where in the US it originated. In the end, we were able to eat some amazing food and dance to some old-school kick back music to just have a great time and embrace our diversity and similarities. It was in that moment that most of us realized that while our grandmas, aunts, uncles, and cousins may prepare a particular meal using a different method, we still connected and bonded during the moments surrounding those meals, like the dancing, playing games, or watching football games. In that moment, we also reminisced on something that reminded us of home. We then started to host community dinners in our dorm hall to share what home would look like along with a better meal than what would be provided in the cafeteria. Food, memory, and hospitality all come together.

4

TRUTH, TRANSPARENCY, AND TRADITION

———

This above all: to thine own self be true.

—WILLIAM SHAKESPEARE[30]

While Hamlet was a tragedy, I think of the meaning of this short quote outlining the importance of being honest in one's ways and relations. As of late, everyone in our society has been speaking their truth, sharing their experiences, sharing the importance of their culture and who they are. I would like to focus quickly on is the part of being honest in our ways and relations. Part of this discussion involves our traditions and culture.

Of course, depending on where you grew up, a minority group almost always lived in the region. Oftentimes that

---

30   William Shakespeare, *Hamlet, Prince of Denmark* (England: 1603) Act I,
     Scene 111, Line 564

minority group got shunned for practicing their traditions and embracing their culture. For example, growing up I'd often bring various Haitian dishes like *diri ak legume* (rice and stew) as my lunch to school instead of a ham and cheese sandwich. (Just so you know, *legume* is a Haitian dish composed of mixed vegetables that are cooked with meat, then mashed and served over rice.) Well, I attended mostly predominately African American private, charter, and public schools K-12, and one of my elementary schools did not have many students that had West Indian or Latino backgrounds, so like most kids, some of the students made fun of how my food looked, but my teacher absolutely loved whenever I would bring my lunches because she understood the love that went into making it, and it smelled and looked amazing to her. She'd often make jokes at the other students and would tell them they didn't know what they were missing.

Now looking back, I sort of wish that I could've taught my fifth-grade class a little bit about Haitian food and culture during lunch and spoken my truth. However, I was embarrassed about it then, and would often ask my mom to make more simple lunches, like the other kids and her response would be, "What's your name?" I'd respond, "Kathiana." She'd follow up by saying, "You're Kathiana, not the other kids. Your lunches have nutrients that their lunches don't have, so be grateful."

I'm certainly grateful now because my lunches were balanced, I did enjoy them, and it did look better than just a sandwich sometimes. If I could go back and talk to fifth-grade me, I would tell myself to speak your truth because it matters and love your Haitian culture because the further you try to distance yourself away from it, the more you'll be reminded of why it's important and why you should embrace that part of you.

Come to find out some of the students in my class did come from a different background and culture and just hid it. So, I could only imagine if we were comfortable enough in our skins and expressed that part of us, how it would shift the conversations and the thoughts of those around us along with some of the friendships that it would bring. Especially since we all enjoy brunches and debates about which dish from our various cultures tasted the best. I'd certainly entertain and participate in some friendly competition and throw-down.

On another note, it wasn't until the 2010 earthquake that I took it upon myself to embrace Haitian culture and resilience, and was able to build a community around other international students at my middle school and share popular Haitian dishes at various diversity nights that I stepped into that truth, because it wasn't welcomed until then. There's something about being different and wanting to share that and making yourself home.

NEW PLACE + OLD SPICE = HOME
Previously, I have mentioned that regardless of where you go a piece of you and a family tradition or recipe follows you. Regardless of where you are from, some things that will always live within you are also memories and past times. I mentioned that I read in a *Global Gastros* article that shared food is understanding, memory, love, and connection. Something that serves us all well is our memories; something that

our memories hold are our traditions, family gatherings, gatherings with friends, outings, barbecues, campfires, and feasts. One thing about tradition is that you can try your hardest to detach or remove yourself from it, but it still is there.

I find that oftentimes assimilating into a new environment can be hard, and if you're the minority it may be hard to express yourself. However, when you're in a new place and you jazz it up with a little bit or a lot of old spice or tradition, you can make that space your home, be comfortable in it, and eventually share a piece of that with others. I remember my mom sharing stories with me of when she first moved to America and how her first experience with American food was Popeyes. She was amazed at how different it was from fried chicken back in Haiti. However, when she and her siblings would have gatherings, they would invite other people who lived in the same apartment complex as them to their gatherings and share some of the island flavor with them. They would absolutely love it. My late Papa Ben would often bring homemade lunches to the factory where he worked and would sometimes share his lunch with others, for someone would always say to him, "Ben, that smells good, what is that, can I have some?" Of course, he would share and that would be a learning moment for the guys who worked with him. He would try his best to explain what the dish was and would always give compliments to the wife and tell them that her cooking was part of why he married her. While my family had to adapt to being in a new space, they strived to share their cultures with others and allowing that exchange to shift the perspective of what Haitian food is and who Haitian people are. An although, they faced judgement from others, they would still be proud of who they are and take the places where they were welcomed and accepted to add to that and make it home.

This reminds me of an article, "How to Maintain Your Culture When Moving to Another Country" on *The Spruce*, by Diane Schmidt. One of the points she shared was the ways of maintaining your culture when moving to another country: staying in touch with people from back home, maintaining cultural traditions, sharing your culture with new friends and colleagues, and volunteering for a nonprofit organization. Two of the shared points that I wanted to draw attention to were maintaining cultural traditions and sharing your culture with new friends and colleagues. As Schmidt shares, "All of us have traditions that we adhere to—events, celebrations and ways of doing things that we grew up with. For children, in particular, maintaining these traditions can help them transition easier to a new culture, knowing that some structure has not changed. At the same time as it's important to maintain the old, don't forget to embrace the new as well. Often, special occasions, holidays, and specific events provide the perfect venue to introduce some of your culture-specific uniqueness to new friends while still embracing the new. . . . Teaching others about your culture is a great way to share what you miss and love about your home while allowing friends and colleagues to get to know you a little better."[31]

During my writing journey, I got the chance to interview Chef Reina Gascon-Lopez, who started a blog surrounding

31   Diane Schmidt, "How to Maintain Your Culture When Moving to Another Country," *The Spruce*, April 11, 2019.

her culinary journey called *The Sofrito Project*. It's called *The Sofrito Project* because *Sofrito* represents her roots, homeland, culture, and people. To her, "It's a labor of love: a project. This is where I share recipes, my thoughts on food culture, and other aspects of life in and out of the kitchen."[32] Through this project, Reina has been able to share dishes that have Latino and Southern influence. Reina was born in Puerto Rico but raised in Charleston, SC, due to her father being in the Navy. She mentioned to me during our interview that when they moved to Charleston, there weren't other Latinos there so, "growing up, one of the things that my family kind of had a hard time adjusting to [was] when we moved. So, it was one of those things that I ended up just doing was embracing my culture and being proud of it. Because we didn't really have a choice but to do that. But, I love sharing my traditional dishes that I grew up eating and I love sharing you know things that I learned culinary school and the dishes that I enjoy eating because I love sharing food with others and I think it's such a huge part of Southern culture. Just like connecting with people and being in the South, food is a huge part of our lives."

FRIED SOUTHERN HOSPITALITY

Reina brought up an interesting point about Southern culture and food. Her comment on the love of sharing food, connecting with other cultures, and that being a part of Southern culture is indeed a fact. Southern hospitality maybe a stereotype, but one of the reasons why people always travel back down to the South or have an inkling to visit is because us Southerners tend to be respectful, warm, sweet, and welcoming to

---

32   Reina Gascon-Lopez, "Who Is Reina," *The Sofrito Project*, 2020.

visitors that come into our homes and treat them like family. Now when you add some Soul and Love to that Southern Hospitality, you win hearts. In my interview with Reina, I asked her to weigh in on the concept of food being connected to our emotions. She shared that "food is a love language because you have to put so much energy and right intention into what you're cooking. So, it could be translated into love and affection when you create a meal and you prepare food for someone else." In the South, when going through your various dining experiences, you typically experience both the love that went into cooking the food when you consume it and the love from those around you that makes you feel at home, especially when trying soul food, down South. Soul food to me is food that was prepared and cooked with tons of love, spice, and tradition, and with classic R&B soul music playing in the background. However, through the help of *The Spruce Eat's* article, "What Defines Authentic Soul Food?" and Britannica, I'll break down what soul food is, what it consists of, and what are its differences to other Southern dishes.

SOUL FOOD BREAKDOWN

Soul Food, the foods and techniques associated with the African American cuisine of the United States. The term was first used in print in 1964 during the rise of "black pride," when many aspects of African American culture—including soul music—were celebrated for their contribution to the American way of life. The term celebrated the ingenuity and skill of cooks who were able to form a distinctive cuisine despite limited means.

Although the name was applied much later, soul food originated in the home cooking of the rural South using locally raised or gathered foods and other inexpensive ingredients. Following their emancipation from slavery in the 1860s, African American cooks expanded on the coarse diet that had been provided them by slave owners but still made do with little. Most of the foods they prepared were common to all the rural poor of the South—light- and dark-skinned alike—but these foods and food-preparation techniques were carried North by African Americans during the Great Migration and thus became identified with African American culture. African Americans were often employed as cooks in white households and in restaurants, and they incorporated the influence of their employers' favored dishes into their home cooking.33

SOUL FOOD REGIONAL OUTLOOK, STAPLES, AND DIFFERENCE FROM SOUTHERN FOOD

Although there were regional variants, such as the Creole influence from Louisiana, many of the same foods were eaten throughout the South. Corn (maize) was raised as a staple, to be ground into cornmeal for cornbread and its local variants hoecakes, baked on a griddle, and hush puppies, usually fried with fish.

---

33   Anita Wolff, "Soul Food," *Encyclopedia Britannica*, accessed February 14, 2020.

Corn also provided hominy grits, to be eaten as a breakfast food or a side dish. Biscuits were a popular form of bread. Rice was an important staple, especially in the Carolinas and in Louisiana. Molasses and a syrup made from sorghum provided sweetening. . . . Freshwater catfish was especially identified with soul food. Vegetables of African origin, such as okra and sweet potatoes, were widely grown, as were melons, greens (including mustard and collards), turnips, cabbage, and beans. Greens, particularly collards, served as important sources of dietary fiber and vitamins. Lima beans, crowder peas, black-eyed peas, butter beans, and green beans were used fresh or dried. Spicy vinegar-based pepper sauce (see chili pepper) remains a widely used condiment. Other popular dishes are fried chicken, short ribs of beef, macaroni and cheese, and potato salad. Desserts include pies and layer cakes, cobblers, and puddings, often incorporating pecans, peaches, and berries.[34]

According to Andrea Lynn from *The Spruce Eats*:

The staples of soul food cooking are beans, greens, cornmeal (used in cornbread, hush puppies, and johnnycakes and as a coating for fried fish), and pork. Pork has an almost limitless number of uses in soul food. Many parts of the pig are used, like pigs' feet, ham hocks, pig ears, hog jowl, and chitlins. Pork fat is

---

34 Ibid.

*used for frying and as an ingredient in slowly cooked
greens. Sweet, cold drinks are always a favorite.*

*To many Americans, all that just sounds like a descrip-
tion of Southern food. The distinctions between soul
and Southern are hard to make. In [Bob Jeffries's] Soul
Food Cookbook (1969), [he] summed it up this way:
"While all soul food is Southern food, not all Southern
food is soul. Soul food cooking is an example of how
really good Southern cooks cooked with what they
had available to them.*[35]

Something along the same lines of Southern hospitality is
that tradition in our culture of wanting to share food with
others oftentimes involuntarily. I can expect to be invited to
someone's Sunday dinner, or having fellowship with other
friends and community members after a church service,
invited over for dinner just because, or hosting dinner at
my house for some family, friends, and their guests.

Similarly, to what Reina mentioned, soul food is prepared
with that love, and people can feel and figuratively taste the
effort that went into preparing the dinner. I bring up soul
food because the African American community is a minority
in various regions of the US and time and time again, they
have tried sharing their culture and traditions with others
and getting in where they can fit in our society.

---

35   Andrea Lynn, "What Defines Authentic Soul Food?" *The Spruce Eats,* July
     3, 2020.

Moreover, the African American community has unknowingly kept the roots of West African cuisine in various ingredients in their dishes. While African Americans were forced into new territory, and they would lose touch of what they were once accustomed to, their traditions and methods of food preparations have evolved through soul food dishes, ingredients, and recipes. Moreover, when I or most think of soul food, we think of home or good times at our grandparents' home. Oftentimes as a community, we host different functions to allow or include others in experiencing soul food dishes or dinners, like a fish-fry at a bingo night, or in honor or reverence for Black History Month, hosting a soul food dinner night. Either way, the African American community has carried out part of their tradition through soul food. It's truly all about having a good time and making yourself home. And no matter what gathering you go to, you leave feeling that way.

MIMOSAS, MILLENNIALS, AND MEETUPS

One way we unknowingly experience the hospitality and foods of various cultures is through our dining experiences. Who doesn't enjoy going to and having brunch? "Crickets chirp-ping," right? Because just like you, I do! And honestly, this can be a friendship breaker, because if I ask any of my friends if they enjoy brunch, they should and probably say that they too enjoy brunch. Brunch is one of those meals that combines everything in one. While I enjoy self-care and being my own best-friend, I find myself not being able to enjoy brunch alone. Now, don't get me wrong. I love quiet dinners followed by a nice aromatic bath to relax after a stressful day. But on a Saturday morning or on a Sunday after leaving church, I almost crave being with friends and enjoying the best part of the weekend . . . Brunch! There's just something about brunch and having the balance of both breakfast and lunch with a group of friends. I looked up why millennials enjoy brunch and in a blog from Satchmo's Grill one of the ten reasons is that "Brunch is more than just a trend; it's a movement. Brunch is an all accepting meal. Brunch doesn't care what you look like or what you're in the mood for. You can go to brunch cute and put together, or a total bum, and brunch will never judge you. Brunch gives you a new opportunity to try your favorite places. Brunch also gives you the best of both worlds—if you are feeling breakfast, or lunch, or both."[36]

What I have enjoyed seeing around this melting pot area that I live in formerly known as the DC metro area is how various cultural restaurants take on the concept of brunch. Your standard American brunch includes an avocado toast; French toast using brioche slices topped with strawberries, syrup, and powdered sugar with a side of bacon; bottomless mimosas; shrimp and grits, and chicken and waffles. However, in DC if you go to Le Diplomate, Dino Gritto, Jaleo, Sopesso, Tupelo Honey, Founding Farmers, Milk & Honey in Smith Commons, Half-Smoke, Texas Jack, or any other brunch-hopping DC brunch spot, you will find that they aim to sell a brunch option that offers different cuisines from all over the world and all around the United States. Whenever, I go to brunch, most of the time I try different things on the menu, and I am almost always content with what I receive. I

---

36   Satchmo's, "Ten Reasons Why We Love Brunch!" *Satchmo's Bar & Grill*, October 20, 2017.

often find that going in a group or bunch and trying various tapas or small plates to share has made those brunches even better, due to the fact that those restaurants strive to share an experience that is similar to a breakfast, lunch, or appetizer in their home country or region. From the plating, seating, and interior design of the restaurant, to the flavor of the food, the chef and owners' goal is to give you and your friends a unique experience.

A TASTE OF A NEW CULTURE WITH A DASH OF TRUTH

This presents the opportunity to break or tear-down an invisible border of a country when you experience their food and hospitality at that restaurant. There's a reason why we all either create or get a list of suggestions of restaurants in your city; so, when others come and visit, they gain an equal experience. They get to step-in and get a glimpse of what it would be like to be in that country or region along with experiencing similar flavors that they either enjoy or would pass on for the next time. As J.R.R Tolkien once said in *The Hobbit*, "If more of us valued food and cheer and song above hoarded gold, it would be a merrier world."[37] Drawing back to the introduction of this chapter, and one's speaking their own truth, tradition and food is one of the simpler ways to express who you are and to share some of your culture and tradition. I won't get into the gastrodiplomatic approach too much here and how to achieve peace in this chapter, but in a later chapter, I will share how to take this concept and shape our relationships both personal and corporate. However, in

---

37   J.R.R. Tolkien, *The Hobbit*, (Houghton Mifflin: Boston, MA. August 15th, 2002), pg 27.

the next chapter I plan on explaining how the concept of tradition, hospitality, and breaking boarders evolves into us forming our community and friendships.

5

COMMUNITY AND FOOD

———

Food is our common ground, a universal experience.

— JAMES BEARD[38]

Food is our common ground because not only do we need it to survive, but various dishes are invented or reinvented and shared on many tables or floors around the world and throughout history. Both our palates and stomachs would agree that no matter where you travel to, food and eating to survive or to enjoying the goodness of a desired dish is a common concept. While every place has its own dining experience, norms, or customs, the meal part of it has become this universal language that people from any part of the world can relate to. Food being placed on various tables around the world forms community and brings people together.

When you hear the word community, what do you think of? I've asked several friends during my writing journey that exact question, and the responses that I would get would

———

38   James Beard, *BrainyQuote.com*, BrainyMedia Inc, 2020.

be: their circle, friends and family, village, kinfolk, student groups, associations, life groups. Like my friends, when I hear the word community, I think of a group of people in different cities that means a lot to me and the joys of hanging out or enjoying their company. Well, the definition of the word community means, "a unified body of individuals: such as the people with common interests living in a particular area broadly..., [or] a body of persons or nations having a common history or common social, economic, and political interests.[39] The definition of the term community has shifted because of how we engage with one another, who we allow into our various circles, how we want to be uplifted, allowing our communities to have safe spaces, and the fellowship that comes from it. The more I spoke to my friends the more I realized that our community or circles are often based on the joys of fellowship. Now, depending on your generation, you may agree to disagree that this is not what matters most when referring to a community. However, I think I've found a definition of community that's more modern thanks to an article written by Fabian Pfortmüller, co-founder of Together Institute, he defined it as "a group of people that care about each other and feel they belong together."[40]

I feel that our first experience of community was often times either formed in our homes or at our school lunch tables. Before I dive into the two, I wanted to share the concept

---

39 *Merriam-Webster.com Dictionary*, s.v. "community (n.)," accessed September 24, 2020.

40 Fabian Pfortmüller, "What does "community" even mean? A Definition Attempt & Conversation Starter," *Medium*, September 20, 2017.

behind family-style dining, how we connect, and how that evolves into us forming our various communities.

According to Liana Robberecht from the Canadian Restaurants and Foodservice News:

> *Family-style dining (also known as English Service) originated long ago with records of such meals dating as far back as Ancient Rome. Invited guests would join around a table for a feast brought in on platters. One can imagine the importance of this shared food and the art of good conversation in such a community-oriented culture. [Now] enter modern-day cuisine. Charcut Roast House in Calgary, Alberta has long been ahead of the family-style dining trend. At their award-winning restaurant, which has focused on family-style dining for over six years, owners/co-chefs John Jackson and Connie DeSousa have been successful in bringing people together to share amazing food and conversation. "Family-style dining invites conversation and sharing, plus you get to try a little bit of everything," says Jackson. "Sometimes perfectly plated food can create silos and can often seem a bit boring. Everyone eats, but you miss out on some of the great conversation, the rituals and the connection that comes with sharing a meal together. When I dine out with friends and family, my favourite part is ordering food for the table that I know we can all enjoy together. We have lots of plates and serving spoons all around, but the conversation is seamless with fond memories that make me smile and say, 'Yeah, I want to eat here*

again.'" Family-style dining is the perfect way to bring people together in the most basic of ways – sharing food. Literally sharing a dish does more than nourish our bodies, it nourishes our souls. Our need for a more real social connection with others has always been expressed in the food and restaurant industry, but this latest trend of sharing takes it to a new level. While food innovation, creativity, technology and style are always moving forward, this "new" trend of sharing food family-style is a way we are moving forward by looking back — and going back — to a simpler, more connected and more social way of eating.[41]

Have you ever thought of why when it's time to eat in grade school, they have us sit either in a circle or at a table to enjoy our different lunches? Well, I have put a lot thought into it, and found that it's part of building friendships and a community around us. Sandra Hinderliter, from Start Empathy, wrote an article about an elementary school in Bridport, Vermont. Bridport Elementary has taught kids the importance of inclusion and empathy toward their peers by creating a system that has the students rotate and sit with different peers every day. Here's how they did it:

Principal Kathleen Kilbourne implemented a system to resolve this classic scene of loneliness and forge new friendships. There's hardly room for the question, "Will you save me a seat?" at Bridport Elementary, where

41   Liana Robberecht, "Family-Style Dining: Bringing People and Food Together," *MediaEdge Communications, Inc.*, August 11, 2016.

students are ushered to assigned tables and given the opportunity to open their hearts and minds to a new friend. Ms. Kilbourne had observed too many days in which the same kids were left out, while the others were constantly accompanied by friends. Something had to change. The school rolled out a new system in which students line up to pick a numbered stick out of a bucket before they get their food. Each stick has a number that corresponds with a table, indicating where they will eat their lunch for the day. This system was implemented less than five months ago. Today, if you strolled into the cafeteria, you wouldn't find any numbers or any sticks. Kilbourne made a promise to the students that the system will eventually fade out if she saw that students learned to value inclusivity and empathy. Kilbourne really witnessed a change a few months in. "A girl was walking around by herself with her lunch in her hand, looking for a place to sit, and four tables asked her to join them. At another table, a kindergartener was sitting alone for just a few moments before two sixth graders came over to sit with him, sparking two others to join and actively include him in conversation," she observed.[42]

Now before you say, "Kathiana, some kids just don't get along, and maybe this won't work," I want you to think of your adulthood and how many tables you sit at and the various connections you make through that. Kids don't remain kids; they grow, and while I'm not an expert in child development,

---

42   Sandra Hinderliter, "Friends at the Lunch Table: Teaching Kids Empathy at School," *The Christian Science Monitor*, February 20, 2014.

I know certain foundations instilled in a kid's early stages tend to play a role in adulthood. Now, most of us don't branch out and sit at various tables until we are either forced to through life, meaning going off to college and meeting new people, moving to a new town, forming new circles, starting a new job internship. We all eventually get out of our comfort zones and form those relationships and friendships and thrive in our various communities. Our greatest exchange is through a meal encounter, and it's beautiful and inspiring to watch communities being built around food. As Sandra mention in her article, "Students and adults all over the country could benefit from an approach in which every person is always welcome at the table in any situation."

I'll never forget stories from one of my former bosses and his trips and dining experiences in Kurdistan or Istanbul and how various business partners or high-level executives would invite him to these dinners that were typically served *Mezze* style. According to a *Spruce Eats* article:

> *Mezze, a style of dining in the Mediterranean and the Middle East, resembles a collection of Spanish tapas and other small plates meant to stimulate your appetite. But unlike those appetizers, mezze often makes up an entire meal, combining both cold and hot, vegetarian and meat items. . . . A truly social event, mezze dining encourages conversation and lingering at the table. The dishes are brought out one by one, first the cold dishes, then the hot. The particular selection of dishes is customized and depend largely on the main course. A main course of fish is accompanied by a*

completely different possible selection of dishes than grilled meats. Sometimes the starters are enjoyed with Raki, an anise-flavored liquor similar to Ouzo. Greek cuisine also has a different, but very related, style of Meze. You may see mezze spelled mazza, meze, mezzah, mezzeh or mezza. It's pronounced mez-ay.[43]

Moreover, my former boss would share how there would be freshly baked flatbreads, homemade hummus, dumplings, salads, perfectly grilled lamb, chicken, vegetables, rice pilaf, grape leaves, pastries, baklava, coffee, teas, and wine. I learned that these dinners were served family-style because the way of business is to form genuine relationships prior to proceeding in shop talk. On the flip side of that exchange, my former boss did have many lifetime friends from these encounters because of how it was presented.

NO LANGUAGE BARRIERS TO OUR TASTEBUDS

This reminds me of an interview that I had with Lauren Bernstein, Founder and CEO of The Culinary Diplomacy Project. She shared with me about the time she took her team to Jordan to learn about Jordanians through their cuisine. "The [Culinary Diplomacy Project], together with chefs Amanda Freitag, Duff Goldman, Mary Sue Milliken, Marc Murphy, and Art Smith, traveled across Jordan to learn about the country's culture through its cuisine. While there, [they] visited Amman, Aqaba, Petra, Wadi Rum, and Irbid experiencing the regional diversity of Jordan. [They] spent

---

43   Saad Fayed, "Middle Eastern Social Mezze Meal," *The Spruce Eats*, March 14, 2019.

time cooking with the local people in their homes, learning their personal stories and traditions through their food. [They] also visited Zaatari Refugee Camp where we paired up with some of the Syrian refugees living there to visit the camp markets together, shopped for groceries and then we returned to their homes to cook together. They shared their food traditions and culture with us as they taught us how to prepare their dishes. We all came back together after cooking to enjoy the meal as a group, the chefs sharing with each other what they had learned."[44]

She shared with me that during this trip, none of them spoke Arabic; however, everyone's taste buds lit up during their various shared dining experiences with the people there and that deepened their connections. Oftentimes when we travel, we try our best to prep ourselves to assimilate to the culture and traditions of that country by trying to learn the language or trying the local versions of that country's cuisine. However, when we get there we may not always know every word, but our dining experiences, and coffee or tea times are always memorable because those flavors aren't a barrier to our taste buds, and sometimes when locals notice that you enjoy their food, you may be lucky to be invited to a dinner or one of their restaurants, which forms a quick bond with that person despite the language barrier. It's amazing to watch how sharing a meal or enjoying a prepared dish can allow you to forget that you have a language difference because of your taste bud's harmony.

---

44 "Out & About," The Culinary Diplomacy Project, October 2019.

NEW PLACE + FOOD + FRIENDSHIP = COMMUNITY

Just as traveling and entering a country has its set of barriers like language, moving to a new place has the same, but there's something about a smiling face or shared meal opportunity that can break that barrier and create community. Living in the Washington, DC metro area can be lonely if you are not a student but a young professional trying to strive in your career. We often can get so zoned into our own bubbles and forget the world around us because we strive for success and want to take the next jump in our careers. I moved to the DC metro area from Atlanta back in 2016 at seventeen years old to attend college at Marymount University (MU). My family was ten hours away, and I knew not a soul in this area. While I am extroverted by nature and made tons of friends during orientation, at times I felt alone. However, I overcame those moments when I got a text from one of my girl or guy friends asking if I would like to tag along to have dinner in the cafe. Now, although sometimes the food would not always be appetizing, we would joke about it, and someone would order from Domino's 2 for $5.99 pizza and brownies menu. We would end up having a great time in our community lounge areas, and I would begin to no longer feel alone. I then joined a church, Capital Life Church (CLC), five minutes down the road from Marymount. They had a young professional group called C3, where we would meet once during the week and sometimes, depending on your small group, on the weekend.

Soon enough, during breaks when I would go home, I would miss that fellowship and interactions with both my friends from MU and CLC. Those friends became my family away from home and have since built my community in the DC

Metro area. I no longer feel alone. A few things that formed this familial relationship was not only common interests but also the concept of breaking bread and breaking borders. I'll never forget my first C3 Friendsgiving. I brought both a traditional Haitian makawoni au graten and my Southern soul baked mac and cheese. The Haitian one was more of a hit than my Southern soul baked mac and cheese because I ran out of cheese and didn't have a car to run back to the store. However, I remember trying various side dishes that represented how it was prepared around the US, which blew my mind. While I hadn't visited those regions of the US, I sort of felt like I was there.

I also remember attending various dinner nights at my small group leaders' home. We would pick a theme and roll with it—for example, California burrito night or Chinese take-out game night. The California burrito night was a game-changer. The California burrito is the standard by which all other massive bricks of Cal-Mex food are measured. It's a jumbo flour tortilla filled with carne asada, guacamole, pico de gallo, cheese, and—setting itself apart from the bean-and-rice base of the Mission burrito—a base of French fries. Take-out game night consisted of us bringing our favorite Chinese take-out entree or side option to dinner, and it was terrific. We had a spread of beef and broccoli, kung pao chicken, basmati rice, lo mein, egg rolls, fried wonton, pot-stickers, and fortune cookies. To jazz the night up a bit, we ended up playing board games and inviting other friends that lived nearby to come eat and hang out. This is a community built on food.

I've said this before, and I'll apply it here again, food is and will always be more than something that curbs or satisfies your hunger. Sharing a meal with friends or strangers brings depth to your community life and shifts your perspective. Our perceptions change once we encounter an exchange that is not our norm that was introduced by a friend or family member. The hospitality component of this exchange plays a more significant role than we acknowledge. Imagine if you attended various events but never felt comfortable or built friendship. You'd probably be miserable. However, if an exchange felt like home and you were welcomed as if you were home, you would want to build a community around that. Your perception of whatever is shared with you there shifts because you take part in it with people you trust.

BUILDING A COMMUNITY/HOMAGE AROUND FOOD

Talk about community and food. I'll never forget when my sister, cousin, and I stood in line for four hours to support a local Atlanta restaurant called Slutty Vegan. Slutty Vegan is a hip counter-serve spot that "aims to destroy the idea a plant-based diet is a bland one, presenting a spread of cuisine event avid carnivores will find quite tempting."[45] We went because we heard not only were the burgers, fries, and drinks free on that given day, but we were moved also by the owner Aisha "Pinky" Cole's story. In 2014, Pinky moved to New York and opened a Jamaican Restaurant called Pinky's. Due to a grease fire, she had to walk away from everything in 2016 and went broke. Fortunately, she got a call to work on a show on the OWN network and built herself back up after the loss. After working hard and rebuilding what was lost, in July of 2018, she came up with a crazy idea to open

---

45 "Slutty Vegan ATL," Roaming Hunger, 2020.

up the restaurant that the world now knows as Slutty Vegan. To Pinky, a slutty vegan "is someone who eats vegan but enjoys junk food—as long as it's not dead. I knew the name would be a great hook to help people reimagine food. [The mission is] to change the narrative on vegan foods, especially in under-informed communities."[46]

As someone who has a parent and family members who too came from the islands and have created their own businesses here in America, I can totally understand when odds are up against you and you start from scratch. Therefore, I was excited to be surrounded by my community at a safe, socially distanced parameter to support and uplift this business. Through the help of special artists, comedians, and shows in Atlanta, they wanted to provide free food to allow people to experience Slutty Vegan. For the restaurant to recover from fake negative reviews posted after a hearsay controversy, these artists all pitched in to support this business on that given day and paid for the city to eat from opening time to closing. So, we happily stood there in line with our number in hand waiting for this experience. I am thinking that since we got there an hour before opening, we would be some of the first few hundreds in the line. I was in the number four-hundred line and a mile away from the entrance.

However, it was not a bad experience. Yes, while our number was in the four-hundred line and we had a mile to walk in the hot sun, we got water, bought ice cream, and waited our turn. I'm amazed at what good food and people can make

46   Micah Solomon, "The Slutty Vegan: Young, African American Founder Pinky Cole's Wild Success with Playful Vegan Food," *Forbes*, July 12, 2019.

you do. When we got close to the front, I'll never forget the music, the dancing, and laughter. Then we were walking up to receive a can of San Pellegrino and take a photo with Pinky, all while quickly receiving our orders for burgers and fries. I was able to share my story and hear others story because hey, what are you going to do for that amount of time but learn more about the people around you. It'll definitely be a memorable day.

One of my favorite movies is *Soul Food*, and in the film Mama Joe, also known as Irma Hall, said, "One finger won't make an impact, but you ball all those fingers into a fist, and you can strike a mighty blow. Now, this family has got to be that fist." Well, Atlanta showed up and showed out that day and blew a mighty blow on the naysayers that have tried to take Pinky and her business out.

DC HUSH SUPPER/UNDERGROUND DINNER COMMUNITY

Earlier this year, one of my work friends gifted me with a ticket to a hush supper dinner, also known as an underground dining experience. The hush supper dinner was definitely a different dinner experience from what I was used to, but it was enjoyable, teachable, and memorable. When you first get there, you have to use the "code word" in your confirmation email to get in. Once the guests were in, we were served cocktails and invited to talk amongst ourselves. We weren't privy to the guest list before attending, which was great because we all had worked in various backgrounds and industries and came from all parts of the world.

Our host, Ghetta, walked us through her family's stories throughout our appetizers at the "Chaat Bar," entree, dessert, and chai. She gave us a history and culture lesson all while entertaining us with some delicious dishes. This in a way formed a community amongst the guests because we all connected that night through food and fun. I still chat with some of the people I met at that dinner till this day. As Ghetta's dinner was different than any dinner that most of us had ever attended, our perceptions changed about dinner culture and what an underground dinner looks like. Whether it's burgers, fries, brunch, or supper, we all can enjoy a dish and learn from someone else's culture and form community around that.

II

6

HISTORY OF FOOD
AND PEACE

———

THE CROSSROADS BETWEEN PEOPLE AND FOOD:
CONCEPT OF THANKSGIVING

One of my favorite American holidays is Thanksgiving.
According to many surveys, almost 50 percent of Americans
would agree that Thanksgiving is also their favorite holiday.
Thanksgiving is one of my favorite holidays because of the
variety of food at the dinner table at three o'clock and the
respect that is established and unsaid at the dinner table or
couches while eating.

A LOOK INTO HISTORY

According to Britannica:

> *Thanksgiving Day, annual national holiday in the
> United States and Canada celebrating the harvest and
> other blessings of the past year. Americans generally*

believe that their Thanksgiving is modeled on a 1621
harvest feast shared by the English colonists (Pilgrims)
of Plymouth and the Wampanoag people. The Amer-
ican holiday is particularly rich in legend and sym-
bolism, and the traditional fare of the Thanksgiving
meal typically includes turkey, bread stuffing, pota-
toes, cranberries, and pumpkin pie. With respect to
vehicular travel, the holiday is often the busiest of the
year, as family members gather with one another.[47]

In 1621, the Plymouth's Thanksgiving began with a few colonists going out "fowling," possibly for turkeys but more probably for the easier prey of geese and ducks, since they "in one
day killed as much as . . . served the company almost a week."
Next, 90 or so Wampanoag made a surprise appearance at
the settlement's gate, doubtlessly unnerving the 50 or so colonists. Nevertheless, over the next few days the two groups
socialized without incident. The Wampanoag contributed
venison to the feast, which included the fowl and probably
fish, eels, shellfish, stews, vegetables, and beer. Since Plymouth had few buildings and manufactured goods, most people ate outside while sitting on the ground or on barrels with
plates on their laps. The men fired guns, ran races, and drank
liquor, struggling to speak in broken English and Wampanoag. This was a rather disorderly affair, but it sealed a treaty
between the two groups that lasted until King Philip's War
(1675–76), in which hundreds of colonists and thousands of
Native Americans lost their lives.[48]

---

47 David J. Silverman, "Thanksgiving Day," *Encyclopedia Britannica.* 2020.
48 Ibid.

This look into history draws me back to one of my favorite shows growing up, *Boy Meets World*. I enjoyed hearing Eric call Mr. Feeny from his porch, watching Corey and Shawn grow in friendship, and witnessing Topanga and Corey's love story. Be it as it may that this show is fiction, I'll never forget their Thanksgiving Day episode. Corey and Shawn arrange for their families to come together for Thanksgiving dinner. During the dinner, let's say Shawn's family didn't have all the fancy hors d'oeuvres and wine that Corey's parents were used to having before Thanksgiving dinner, but Shawn's step-mom, Virna, aimed to level up to their standard by serving them Cheez Whiz, Rice Chex, and olives with pimento, and sangria with bananas and oranges to impress the Matthews. (Now for those who have never watch the show, you'll say to yourself okay now what's the point here. While the show was filmed in the late '90s, the producers pointed out that there was an unsaid issue between class in Philadelphia, Pennsylvania. Corey comes from a two-parent home whose parents were both educated and had good-paying jobs. Shawn, on the other hand, lives in a trailer with his father and stepmom.)

However, while they attempted to enjoy a disastrous dinner, Shawn's father, Chet, gets called into an emergency meeting with the Trailer Park Homeowners Association. In this meeting, they tell Chet that he needs to get rid of the "outsiders." So, he then tries to get rid of the Matthews but is then succumbed by the bond of Corey, Shawn, and other friends that lived in the Trailer community. The most moving part of that scene was that the kids kept telling others that there's always room at their table. They did not let their differences divide them from having a meal or enjoying each other's friendship and company.

This situation led Shawn to write a shockingly A+ paper. Sharing how he spent Thanksgiving "with the Hutus and the Tutsis." (Just in case you didn't know, the Hutus and Tutsis go back to the Rwandan genocides. "The split between Hutus and Tutsis arose not [due to] religious or cultural differences, but economic ones. Hutus were people who farmed crops, while Tutsis were people who tended livestock. Most Rwandans were Hutu. Gradually, these class divisions became seen as ethnic designations.")[49] This was a real surprise to him, because he lived in Philadelphia and thought that kind of prejudice based on class differences "only happened in undeveloped countries." But he discovered that people can be just as undeveloped and just as cruel even in his civilized country. However, what gave him hope is that as long as children are educated about the dangers of prejudice and intolerance, "perhaps there will be a reason for Thanksgiving in the future."

As I shared earlier in the book, my family came from Haiti and being first-generation, a lot of American traditions and holidays were a learning experience for my family. Fortunately, my uncles married some amazing Southern Black wives who can help cook up a fantastic Thanksgiving dinner. My maternal grandparents had nine kids, and I am one of the forty-one grandkids. Throughout the years, our Thanksgiving dinners have been vast, and we have not had one table big enough for us to gather around or to split adults vs. kids. However, it's easy for us to sit around the couch to watch college football or play games or overhear my mom's

---

49 Beauchamp, Zack, "What You Need To Know about The Rwandan Genocide," *Vox,* April 10, 2014.

twin Uncle P cracking jokes in the kitchen about a dish or a pastime. In the past, you'd find my late grandma schooling us grandkids or family friends in dominoes. You'd see kids running around, and my mom and aunties laughing around the table sharing past times or gossip. I have a great time during Thanksgiving because although my family may disagree on politics, sports teams, game strategies, or family issues, these are not discussed, and the meal exchange is much greater than the underlying tension.

I'll never forget while watching one of my favorite movies *Soul Food*, hearing Mama Joe (Irma Hall) saying, "One finger won't make an impact, but you ball all those fingers into a fist, and you can strike a mighty blow. Now, this family has got to be that fist."

Our family gatherings come together beautifully because of our differences. Fortunately for us, they include a fusion between the Caribbean, Latin, and Southern soul food and flavor. We often have both a brown-sugar butter oven-roasted turkey sitting next to Haitian fried turkey; eskovet fish sitting next to my Auntie Marie's famous shrimp stew; curry goat sitting next to collard greens that were made using turkey neck or ham hocks. Southern macaroni sits next to Haitian makawoni au graten. Southern pecan pie sits next to my mom's pein patat or my Aunt Carole's red velvet. The food list goes on and on, but the harmony that fuses the two cuisines is beautiful. The flavor appeals to your palate, and everyone enjoys everything Thanksgiving dinner has to offer. However, after saying grace and sitting down at the table or across each other on the couch watching college football, we all strike the blow of understanding one another and setting our differences, so then the concept of ubuntu also begins to happen.

UBUNTU AND EMOTIONAL INTELLIGENCE

In my introduction, I mention that *ubuntu,* meaning I am because you are and you are because I am, can begin to happen while exchanging a meal. Looking back, before being introduced to the concept of ubuntu, I believe that my mom and my late grandmother taught me this concept. Moreover, I see this playing out through the exchange of Thanksgiving dinner.

I learned about this concept through one of my former United Nations Association advisors, Soonhoon Ahn. She's a lifelong advocate of international development careers for professionals seeking to advance human life quality. During this book's writing process, I got the chance to interview Soonhoon. During my interview, I remember her telling me that the ubuntu concept means so much to her because she noticed the importance of understanding each other. She said, "It's far more important than listening to somebody. Sometimes, it is understanding someone."

While I understand the importance of listening and understanding someone, this didn't come clear to me until she mentioned emotional intelligence.

She shared her story of when she first moved to the United States from South Korea and how certain conversations evolved due to mutual connections or interest. She said, "Whenever somebody says, 'I enjoy eating Korean food,' instantly, my mind is open and receptive to starting a conversation with that person." For she believes that "If you enjoy my food, and I enjoy yours, how can we be different." She explained how this not a logical reaction, but it is more of an emotional response and identity. Due to her career, she mentioned that "nowadays we talked about emotional [quotient] EQ more than [intelligence quotient] IQ, but people don't realize that now it is emotional intelligence that allows us to connect with people. It's not all about how I feel [or] what I feel. In a way, it is opening up and understanding: how someone is to you, how that you think that person is shifting their own norm and opening up for you. Rather than walking away and not connecting."

After having the interview with Soonhoon, I decided to look into emotional intelligence to get a better understand of that term. The term *emotional intelligence* means "the capacity to be aware of, control, and express one's emotions and handle interpersonal relationships judiciously and empathetically." Emotional intelligence is often broken down into four domains: "1) Self-Awareness as the foundational capacity of how emotions affect the self and others; 2) Self-Management as the balance of emotions toward goal attainment; 3) Social Awareness as the fostering of connection and understanding of others; and 4) Relationship Management as the interaction with others for the greatest impact."[50]

---

50 Belinda Chiu, et al., "Mindful Diplomacy: The Case for Emotional Intelligence in Leadership," *Key Step Media*, 2020.

EMOTIONAL INTELLIGENCE + WINE = BEST HAPPY HOUR

My former colleague, Veaceslav Pituscan, a former Moldovan diplomat, shared with me that he served as a career diplomat for twenty-three years. During that time, he had a chance to talk to foreign diplomats that had an assignment in Moldova, and one thing that they always mentioned when they were starting conversation was how great Moldovan wine tasted. Moldova is famous for their wine and the kind of model and brand that it's becoming now, is enormous. Therefore, they would often say "it is so good, what is the secret."

Veaceslav told me that he'd oftentimes say that the secret lies in the story of the underground Moldovan wine cities formally known as "Mileștii Mici's wine cellar near one of the well-known wineries named the Cricova winery." The 50-year-old Mileștii Mici's wine cellar has been recognized by the Guinness Book of World Records as the largest wine collection in the world by number of bottles. Veaceslav went on to tell me that the length of the underground cellar runs over 150 miles long, so you have to take your car because that too long of a walk for a proper wine tasting. Within the city, several streets are named after different types of wines. He said that this is one of the top reasons behind tourism in Moldova since 2013 and why he appreciates the efforts of the former U.S. Secretary of State John Kerry in 2013 in creating a form of "wine diplomacy."

With the help of Secretary Kerry in 2013, wine tourism was able to be restored and thrive again. In 2013, John Kerry was the first U.S. secretary of state to visit Moldova in more than two decades. During this visit he held a press conference in the underground wine city and pledged to support Moldova's pro-Western moves in the face of Russian pressure.

Quick backstory, Russia imposed sanctions on Moldova because they signed an association agreement with the European Union. Therefore, Russia decided to establish an embargo on Moldovan wines and beverages that used to be exported to Russia, due to the "good soil" in Moldova. This made it difficult for Moldova to be economically stable because this was one of the main exports that caused their economy to thrive. They established this embargo on Moldovan wine and food to make it harder for the country to grow economically as it can cause potential partners and stakeholders like the European Union to not engage in policy conversation with Moldova or aid them in this very difficult situation.

Russia responded to Moldova's moves toward Brussels by cutting off imports of Moldovan wine. Wine sales to Russia have been an important source of revenue for the country of about 3.5 million people, which is the poorest in Europe. In announcing its ban on imports of Moldovan wines and spirits in September of 2013, Russia said they contained impurities and that Moldova had consistently failed to act to improve the quality of its produce. Kremlin critics said that the previous Russian bans on wine from Moldova and Georgia had been politically motivated. Then US officials said that the State Department would be working with the European Union (EU) to help the Moldovan wine industry find new markets.[51]

A senior State Department official said Russia should see the benefits of closer ties between its neighbors and the EU. "We have been very clear with the Russians that we don't see any need to see the decision of Moldova and Georgia to initial agreements with the EU as a zero-sum game, and that we think that kind of play is self-defeating," the official said. "If Russia's neighbors become richer and more prosperous as a result of having visa liberalization to the European Union and increased trade, they are more able to buy more things from Russia as well, and they are more stable on Russia's periphery." Russian sanctions against Moldova were "a matter of concern" given Moscow's membership of

---

51   David Brunnstrom, "Kerry Visits Western-Leaning Moldova to Show Support," *Reuters*, December 4, 2013.

the World Trade Organization, the official said, but added that it would be up to the Moldovans to decide whether to raise a complaint at the world trade body. Therefore, the EU had reduced, then dropped all its tariffs on Moldovan wine in response to the Russian move. [52]

So, at Cricova, "Kerry unveiled a new marketing logo for Moldovan wine and said the United States would sponsor Moldovan wine growers to allow them to visit America to explore new markets. Moldovans describe Cricova as the largest wine cellars in the world, with 120 km (75 miles) of tunnel-like storage galleries. I strongly feel that emotional intelligence is what struck the former U.S. Secretary of State John Kerry in 2013. Essentially, this is how emotional intelligence and wine won the heart of world leaders, leading them to create peace in forming some of the best happy hour possibilities in Moldova."[53]

GRANDPA KITCHEN

While wine is amazing, winning because of wine is even better. This concept of food and peace is seen today through the works of the late Narayana Reddy, a seventy-three-year-old Indian cook whose YouTube channel, *Grandpa Kitchen*, garnered more than six million followers with videos of him preparing gargantuan amounts of food to feed orphaned children and other hungry people. The late Mr. Reddy, formally known as Grandpa Kitchen, would share with the world videos that followed a straightforward formula: adorable

---

52 Ibid.

53 Ibid.

children, heartwarming music, inspirational sayings, and large amounts of food. He brought a new meaning to Pitmaster because he would often cook outside over an open fire to prepare mountains of chicken and lamb biryani and enough macaroni and cheese to fill an inflatable kiddie pool. Several times, he made pizzas the size of small trampolines using large pots and pans, and another time he made mini chocolate doughnuts that would put a smile on the faces of all the children that would receive or partake in this meal.

The food Grandpa prepared would always represent different culinary traditions, and he invariably grinned as he explained the recipes and prepared the food. Episodes began with the motto "Loving. Caring. Sharing. This is my family." This shares the understanding that food is more than just satisfying one's hunger. Sharing food can relay the emotions of love, care, and family.

FOOD IS . . .

One of my all-time favorite non-super bowl commercials is the snickers commercial with the tagline "You're not you when you're hungry." Food is more than what we perceive it to be. Food is more than satisfying our cravings or ridding of our hunger pains. Food is love, joy, memory, identity, connection, creation, art, and understanding, which causes some form of peace amongst the human race.

We don't just use food to satisfy our own needs; we also use food to sometimes show an emotional connection with others. From our first sample of our mother's milk to our grandmother's homemade chicken or oxtail stew, food is a way we connect and show love for others. Let's be serious. You know a relationship is getting real when your partner invites you over to meet the family and share a home-cooked meal. When a best friend is dumped, we rush over with ice cream and brownies and console them over the situation. We also show a sort of affection or care when a neighbor or friend suffers a loss by bringing them casseroles, fried chicken, rolls, pound cake, pie, and sweet tea. Maybe that's a Southern thing, but you get my point. Food is then a catalyst of love, connection, and understanding.

Preparing and sharing food with people you love solidifies the connection you have due to it forming a memory. Because we apply so much emotional importance to food in the moment, it only makes sense that it would also become an important part of our memories. Studies have shown that our recollection come easily and clearly when they are attached to a physical sensation as well as an emotional experience. From the sounds of cheers from a crowd to the feeling of something tangible, when we use our five physical senses, we create stronger memories. Food holds some connections to memory and history.

No wonder so many of our memories are attached to food. Perhaps it is a memory of baking homemade cookies with your grandma, making pancakes with your dad for breakfast, enjoying a great meal shared with some close friends or just recalling the delicious gelato you had during your trip in Italy with your friends or partner. Food has the ability to activate multiple senses—smell, sight, and of course taste—to help us remember some of life's most meaningful and magical moments, whether large or small.

Food is also an identity. The human race has always placed strong importance on cultural identity and making it known to the world their pride to that identity. In the past, being able to identify someone to a tribe or as belonging to one group or another was an issue of safety and security. The question of "are they a friend or a foe" did not rely on an individual person but rather their identity as part of a group. Therefore, food, in turn, became a way of quickly identifying people. Today, food is a way to connect to your heritage and to your own cultural identity, whether that means me and my family enjoying a plate with rice and beans, plantains, chicken stew, a spicy slaw in Haiti or a new Latino family in the United States having twelve grapes on New Year's Eve, for good luck into the New Year, that is one identifying with their culture.

Whether people stay home and test out recipes that have been passed down generations—making old family recipes with their grandmothers—or move halfway around the world and still keep their cherished recipe ingredients "from the home country," food is a way to identify who you are, where you come from, and the history of your people.

Food being a way we culturally identify validates the claim of food also being a connection:

> *When you think about it, in the history of mankind, eating alone was never something truly normal. Perhaps a hunter would snack while out alone in the forest, but meals were always something shared. Families and friends would gather together to eat. All major social events seemed to include food, from weddings to funerals. Today, with the way technology and work culture creates physical isolation, eating alone is much more common but even so, people seek out others to enjoy a meal with—to connect with. Connecting with friends and family around good food. While food is often used to separate us into different groups, it can also be used to connect us. When you go on a first date, what is the most likely situation? Dinner, right? Or if not that at least a cup of coffee at a cafe. The picturesque image of the happy family always seems to show them sitting around a dinner table. Even in the business world, connections are made over coffee or a business meeting lunch. Connection and inclusion is an important human need; isolation is one of the top causes of depression. Combining that need for connection with another basic human need—food—ensures*

not only our physical health but our emotional health
as well.[54]

Food is understanding. As the famous cookbook author James Beard said, "Food is our common ground, a universal experience." It doesn't matter if you are Black, White, or Brown: You eat. It doesn't matter if you are Christian, Buddhist, or Muslim: You eat. The foods we eat around the world are vastly different, but the connection we have with food and the act of eating is something we can all relate to. This universality allows food to create a true opportunity for universal understanding." When you realize that a father or mother halfway around the world just wants to provide and feed his children like any other good parent you can connect with them on a deeper level. You see this across cultures, the use of food to solidify an understanding between people. We literally speak of peace being created with the "breaking of bread." When people come together over food, they can better relate to each other, whether that means a family trying to form better bonds of understanding or enemies trying to forge a new peace.

Food is art. There is a beauty in old family recipes. Passed down from generation to generation, these pieces of the past connect us with our heritage and helps with our identity. "At the same time though, food for mankind has always represented progress, change, and invention. From the first days of agriculture to

54 "The Role Of Food In Human Culture · Global Gastros," *Global Gastros*, 2018.

the molecular gastronomy trends of today's top restaurants, food has always shown the true ability of the human imagination. Food as an art form and a way to express creativity and imagination. Think about it. What would Italian food be without tomatoes? And yet, this crucial ingredient was only introduced to Europe a few hundred years ago. The success of the human species relied on our ability to adapt, change, and create, especially when it came to food sources. Food is both nutrients and art. Today, we continue to stretch our minds and abilities from the creation of new hit street foods to fine dining restaurants pushing the realm of what is food further and further to the future.[55]

Food is also joy. If you are like myself or any of my family and friends, you can agree that food brings you joy. Enjoying food makes sense in terms of being excited for a meal or eating to survive. Think about it. If we didn't have a strong desire or drive to eat, we would not only always be "hangry," but we would also starve to death. Therefore, we do our best to make our meals flavorful enough to satisfy our palates to bring ourselves joy and to continue to survive. Food does not just make us happy and satisfied but often gives us true joy. Throughout history, the wealthiest of society would have their wealth shown through great banquets and feasts. In the same way art and music would signify "the good life," so would food. Food was about living well and enjoying life. In reality though, the cost of the feast or the rarity of the ingredients

---

55   Ibid.

mattered little. Does that sound like our brunches today? I thought so.

So, anyone who has enjoyed the comfort of a peach cobbler or a chicken pot pie or pot roast on a cold day knows the simple, peaceful joy food can bring. "When you eat something that just tastes so perfect that it literally reminds you to stop and appreciate all you have in your life—that is the unique joy and magic of good food."[56] There is joy in simple, fresh ingredients in homemade recipes.

Food and food culture quite obviously make up an important part of who we are, how we connect, what we value, and how we express ourselves as people. As our world becomes more and more interconnected, as people move across the globe, and as Western culture becomes more popular, the food and food culture landscapes of our world will continue to change and evolve. "Change is inevitable, but it is important to honor and acknowledge the ways we have all personally grown and been shaped by our own unique food cultures."[57] Perhaps it is time to learn to make your grandmother's famous stew or to write down the story of the first homemade meal you cooked for your partner or spouse, even if it did involve not properly reducing the wine in your pasta sauce or spilled red wine on your counter. It all serves as a memory and shows us that at the end food is more.

---

56 Ibid.

57 Ibid.

7

THE SAVORY SHIFT

———

The human frame being what it is, heart, body, and brain all mixed together, and not contained in separate compartments as they will be no doubt in another million years, a good dinner is of great importance to good talk. One cannot think well, love well, sleep well, if one has not dined well.

—VIRGINIA WOOLF

There is POWER in our PALATES. Just as our tongues linguistically can have "the power of life and death."[58] Our palates, or tastebuds, also have the power to shift our opinions (brain), appreciation (heart), and outlook (view/body) of other dishes from different cultures. Our dining experiences affects our likes or dislikes of dishes or another dining customs. Whether it be the flavor of the food, the service at the restaurant, or the traditions of how the food is served, our perceptions of various dishes can be formed from either a good or bad dining experience, or not formed in our hesitation to try new dishes because we try to avoid dishes that

---

58   Proverbs 18:21

might taste bad to us. While I don't like speaking for everyone, I think we can all agree that we have had our picky moments when you say to ourselves, if it's up to me, I will never eat "X" again. However, as we travel, wine and dine at new restaurants, and come across new recipes, unless we are allergic to an ingredient, we tend to try new things and our palates begin to shift.

Personally, it wasn't until my adulthood that I started to enjoy eating things that I didn't enjoy as a child. For example, potatoes regardless of form—mashed, shredded, fried, roasted, baked—I disliked it all. However, this changed when I was an undergrad at Marymount through one of my dinners with some friends from my Rowley Hall group chats. We would meet up in the dining hall or another dining spot on campus called Bernie's. One day, after being on the go all day and not stopping to eat, I became hungrier than usual around dinner time. I'll never forget that on this day, they were serving fried chicken in the dining hall, with veggies, mashed potatoes, and salad options. I thought to myself that, I needed something aside from a salad to balance out the fried chicken. So, after sharing my thoughts with my friends Paula and Leah, they highly suggested that I try the mashed potatoes. "It won't kill you, and for Marymount, it's good," they promised. So, I did, and for a Sodexo Marymount dish—I promise, I'm not throwing shade, most of our dining hall dishes weren't tasty—it was pretty good.

Later that night, I began to question why I would judge those who enjoyed mashed potatoes or the number of times I'd toss French fries because I didn't want to give it a chance unless it was sweet potatoes. On that particular day, my outlook and opinion started to change. Also, thanks to that particular meal exchange, it allowed that moment to happen. Believe it or not, I now make a mouthwatering and aromatic rosemary garlic confit mashed potato (recipe in chapter 9), tasty breakfast potatoes, killer loaded potatoes, and more. I also now appreciate that exchange far more now than when they suggested. Little did I know it would lead to a more significant impact in my acceptance of other dishes that I usually wouldn't prefer or learn which potatoes are best for which dish.

Now you're probably wondering why I disliked potatoes so much. I didn't like the texture or flavor and was often forced to eat them. My late grandma was sweet but also your traditional old-school grandparent that didn't play during meal times. Mostly because of the time to prepare the dish, the love she poured into it, and the cost to make it, she expected everything to be off of your plate by the end of breakfast, lunch, or dinner. She had a golden rule that you couldn't get up from the table without finishing everything on your plate. To not finish your food or mentioning that you did not like it was a sign of disrespect to her. While I wasn't a picky kid, I truly didn't like potatoes and would refuse to eat them. So, whenever she would make one of my least favorite Haitian dishes, called *Bouillon* similar to the Latin American dish *Sanchoco*, I would get a lot warnings and bribes. Just so you know, Bouillon is a chicken or beef soup/stew that contains potatoes, yucca, carrot, dumplings, plantains, and other root vegetables.

Now looking back, I wish I could go back and just eat it all and not give her such a hard time because it's not that bad.

Honestly, now when my mom makes it, I sometimes look forward to it.

I now find that my late grandma was right about the love, time, and cost it took to prepare our meals. Similar to my grandma, now that I cook and often entertain friends and family, I would feel the same way if my family or guest didn't eat what I prepared because they were picky or wouldn't give it a try. I would also question my cooking capabilities or the ingredients that I use. While I'm a home chef, I think anyone that makes anything from a simple dish to a five-course meal can agree that you prepared it all with love. We can also agree that you spent time preparing it to attempt to make it taste appetizing. So, I've learned that there should be a sense of reciprocal respect that occurs during a meal exchange.

MINDFUL MEALS

This reminds me of a conversation with my friend Manal about Pakistani cuisine. We were talking about hosting our friends and providing them with traditional dinners. I asked her what goes through her mind when she invites friends for a traditional Pakistani dinner. So, she shared with me that "it takes a lot of preparation. If I were hosting guests or friends on a weekend, I would start a few days early. I would like to have my menu down or to be considerate of people's dietary restrictions. One of the great things about Pakistani food is that you can enjoy it even if you are vegetarian, as I am vegetarian and still enjoy my mom's recipes." I mentioned to her that oftentimes when we do host, part of it is being considerate of everyone's tolerance and accommodating our menus for everyone.

So, Manal went on to share about hosting a group of her friends of various backgrounds for dinner when she lived in Madrid. She said, "I remember one time back when I was living Madrid, Spain, and I had friends from different backgrounds, and it was always nice coming together. I had two friends visiting who I had known at Berkeley and they were both visiting Madrid at the same time, and so I had them over plus a couple of my friends that I'd made in Madrid. Since they were coming over, I made like a vegetarian Pakistani feast." I love recreating dishes or moments, so I asked her how did she create this feast? Her reminiscing and sharing were torture because I got hungry. But she said, "Several of them were vegetarian. So, I made a delicious beetroot curry. Oh my god, it's really good! It's basically beetroots cooked in cloves, cinnamon, ginger, chilies, and coconut. I then made a big pot of delicious orange lentils. Then made a spinach and potato curry, and an eggplant curry. So, there were several different vegetables to eat. Once everything was ready, we set the table and added the nice napkins. Then enjoyed sitting down and eating this fantastic meal."

Her biggest win that night was that they all really enjoy everything on the table. Some of her friends complemented her by saying "We've never seen these kinds of dishes in Pakistani restaurants nor did we ever realize how yummy vegetarian food can be or vegetables in general." She went on to share how special that night was, and I saw the love, time, and passion that went into creating that wonderful feast. She later shared with me that it also gave her a sigh of relief that they all enjoyed it.

So, I asked her why did she think that they would not enjoy it? Manal shared with me that she'd often invite her Pakistani friends over for a homemade dinner because she felt like "they can then they can appreciate it the right way." Because when she would have other non-Pakistani friends over for dinner "there's been the issue of like: this person not liking cilantro, someone else not liking spicy foods, or another person who can't tolerate spices." She went on to say that, "one thing like that is very like essential to make any dish tasty, especially Pakistani cuisine are your use of spices and herbs."

I too cook and enjoy Southern soul food, Haitian, Latin, and other international dishes, so I cosigned her statement. The flavor of what you're eating needs to be present and adding herbs and spices makes a big difference. However, just in case you were wondering, Manal shared with me that Pakistani cuisine often contains cilantro and mint. So, she often thinks maybe she can alter things, but the flavors aren't all there, and it ends up not tasting the same. Manal then mentioned that, "This is the reason why a lot of restaurants end up dumbing down like a culture's cuisine, to kind of suit the local palate." While she understands the reasoning behind it, which I get why they do that, she feels people should be exposed to it like in the most authentic way possible and should adapt their palate to the dish. Moreover, restaurants that try to please their customers and business opportunities by holding back on true experience are doing us a greater disservice than service.

PLEASING AND TEACHING

While I understand the importance of making things familiar so that your guest or customer will enjoy their meal or be more receptive of ingesting what you prepared or what they order, we should allow homemade meals or restaurant-made meals to share their stories and tell their truth. Remember how in chapter 4, I spoke about the importance of being true to you and speaking your truth? Well, whenever you prepare homemade meals for your friends, the best way to speak your truth is tangibly through the flavors of the dish and the spices that you use.

Chef Saul Montiel of Cantina would agree with my statement, for he recently did an interview with *NowThis* and shared the truth about true Mexican cuisine instead of the perception of Mexican food in America. According to Chef Saul, "People's perception of Mexican food is very different from actual authentic Mexican food. Nothing from Taco Bell (which was named the number one Mexican restaurant in the country in a recent national survey) resembles actual food eaten in Mexico."[59]

He added to that by saying, "I think what Taco Bell is doing and some other brands are taking Mexican and commercializing it and that's okay, but at the same time we are losing our history, we're losing our culture, we're losing who we are as Mexican cuisine," he explained. "You know, besides those hard-shell tacos, go and order a gordita with burrata. In our menu we have gordita with burrata and heirloom tomatoes,

---

59 *NowThis*, "Everything You Know about Mexican Food Is a Lie," Group Nine Media, Inc., October 16, 2018.

so it's old school and new school, but don't be afraid, nothing is going to happen. If you don't like, it, you send it back."[60]

Now I know all restaurants and many people that make a homemade meal and host family and friends hold back on the authenticity of the dish that they prepare and serve. However, it's important for it to be both a pleasing and teaching experience because your palate learns to adapt to those flavors, and you're enjoying or taking in what another culture aside from your own has to offer. In those moments when your palate shifts and you either enjoy or not enjoy those new flavors that you get a 360 degree view and experience.

THE SHIFT

The 7 reasons why it's important to let our palates shift are:

1. "Trying and falling in love with new flavors."[61]
2. "Taking in a wide variety of nutrients from varied sources."[62]
3. "To keep our minds growing, evolving, and learning about our food."[63]
4. "To impress our family and friends when they're over for dinner—haha, kidding! sort of? In all honesty though,

---

60 Ibid.

61 Kelly Maia Agnew, "7 Reasons Why It's Important to Explore New Food," Kelly Maia Nutrition, 2020.

62 Ibid.

63 Ibid.

you become an example to them, and can encourage them to adopt an open mind, too!"[64]

5. "It's a form of being adventurous in the comfort of your home or at a local restaurant. Isn't being adventurous supposed to be rewarding?"[65]

6. "It's an opportunity to broaden your 'food' spectrum, giving you more options for meals, snacks, and more."[66]

7. It inspires you to travel and take on new challenges.

Ultimately, we are all entitled to our own opinions but should try to exemplify a level of reciprocal respect during our dining experiences. So, let's challenge our palates and allow them to shift during our various dining experiences. In the end, our goal is to enjoy new bites, share mutual respect, and learn about new cultures and dishes that pique our interest.

---

64 Ibid.
65 Ibid.
66 Ibid.

8

SEASONAL SPREADS

Preparing and serving food had always been a joy, for it made her appreciate the abundance of the world.

—ELIZABETH CAMDEN[67]

Does anyone remember dinner time when we were kids, and our job was to set the table or help prepare the meal to put on the table? Well, I do and aside from watching or attempting to help my mom, setting the table was my favorite part. I'll never forget the time I got to help cook and set up the appetizer, entree, and dessert table for my grandmother's eightieth birthday party. One thing I enjoyed making that day was the fruit platter. Originally, my mom wanted diced fruit on a tray for people to take a fork and take their pieces of fruit. While that idea was perfectly fine, I decided that it needed to look better than diced fruit on a tray.

---

67 Elizabeth Camden, *Until the Dawn*, (Bloomington, MN: Bethany House Publishers, 2015), 39.

So, I purchase some ice cream scoopers and cookie ballers. I purchased watermelon, cantaloupe, green grapes, blueberries, and strawberries, along with mint leaves as garnish. After rinsing my berries and grapes, I sliced the watermelon, cantaloupe, and strawberries in half. I then pitted the cantaloupe and began scooping out cute cantaloupe balls and placing then in a bigger bowl. Afterward, I took my ice cream scooper and began to scoop watermelon balls and place those in another bowl. I then noticed that my strawberries were too big, so I cut them into fourths instead. Afterward, I took the round platter and began layering the fruit. In the first platter, I let the blueberries be the base then added the grapes and strawberries around the edges for color play, then the cantaloupe balls. I topped it off with a couple of watermelon balls and mint leaves. The other platter started with the watermelon balls forming my base with the remaining strawberries going around the edge of the watermelon balls, then cantaloupe; afterward, I added the remaining grapes and topped it off with the remaining blueberries. Both platters were so beautiful that some people at the party asked if I could make them fruit platters for their personal gatherings. Also, it was easier for someone to stick a toothpick into the fruit and get what they want instead of scooping it out.

As simple as fruit may be, its convenience, beauty, and flavor on a platter is something that some look forward to at a gathering or party. Personally, there's something about flavor, conventionality, and eye-pleasing foods that makes my heart happy at any social event. Now, I understand at family gatherings we have big spoons and forks that you help yourself with, but I'm thinking that post COVID-19, people will be more reluctant to keep touching the same big spoon or fork to help themselves. So, I've come up with a couple of appetizer, salad, entree, dessert, and cocktail recipes based on seasons where they can easily be pre-plated or pre-cut so everyone's not touching everything. Feel free to mix and match them up as everyone likes eating or trying different things.

FOOD PREPARATIONS AND CULTURE

FOUR SEASON PREPARATIONS

APPETIZERS

WINTER

Cranberry Balsamic Orange Honey Goat Cheese Appetizer (Inspired by Laura, Joy, Food Sunshine)

INGREDIENTS:
- 1 tablespoon of balsamic vinegar
- 3 tablespoons orange-blossom honey divided (regular clove honey works as well)
- 1 cup fresh cranberries, divided
- 2 teaspoons orange zest
- ¼ cup of pecans, chopped
- ½ tablespoon of butter
- 2 teaspoons granulated sugar or turbinado sugar
- 1/8 teaspoon ground cinnamon
- Pinch of pink Himalayan salt
- 1 8-ounce of log goat cheese
- 1 pound of love

INSTRUCTIONS:

Step 1: Pecans

Line a baking sheet with wax paper, set aside.

Melt butter in a small saucepan over medium heat.

Add pecans, granulated sugar, cinnamon, and salt, and stir to combine.

Cook, stirring constantly, until the pecans are coated and begin to become darker brown,

about 3-4 minutes

Remove from heat and spread on wax paper to cool.

Step 2: Cranberries

In a small saucepan over medium heat, add 2 tablespoons of the orange-blossom honey and the balsamic vinegar and heat until combined (about 30 seconds).

Add ½ cup of fresh cranberries and cook on medium heat for about 3 minutes until you begin to hear them pop, stirring occasionally.

Mash the cranberries with a potato masher or fork with some love.

Continue cooking until the mixture begins to thicken and resemble jelly.

Add the remaining 1 tablespoon of the orange-blossom honey and ½ cup cranberries and stir to combine.

Continue cooking and stirring occasionally until the mixture becomes thick and the cranberries just begin to pop (do not mash them this time).

Remove mixture from heat and let stand at room temperature for 10 minutes or until ready to serve.

Step 3: Assemble

Place goat cheese on a cheese board or serving plate.

Gently stir pecans into the cranberry mixture.

Carefully spoon the mixture on top of the goat cheese log, spreading it evenly, drizzle orange-blossom honey, garnish with rosemary, then serve with your favorite crackers!

SPRING

Strawberry Baked Brie (Inspired by Jennifer Debth's Yummy Recipe)

INGREDIENTS:
- 2 tablespoons of balsamic vinegar
- 2 tablespoons of orange-blossom honey
- ½ pint of strawberries, sliced
- ¼ cup of fresh basil minced

- 1/3 cup of pecans or walnuts, toasted and roughly chopped
- 1 8-ounce round of Brie cheese
- Sliced toasted baguette for serving

INSTRUCTIONS:

In a medium sized bowl, mix together balsamic vinegar and honey together until well combined.

Place the sliced strawberries into the mixture, stir to coat the strawberries, and let sit in the fridge for about 10 minutes.

Preheat oven to 375 F and line a rimmed baking sheet with a silicone mat or parchment paper and place cheese in center.

Bake on middle rack until cheese feels very soft when pressed, about 15 minutes.

Remove strawberries from fridge and stir in fresh basil and pecans.

Top brie with strawberry mixture and serve immediately with toasted baguette slices!

Melon and Prosciutto Skewers (Inspired by Lauren Miyashiro's Delish Recipe)

INGREDIENTS:

- Skewers
- 1 cantaloupe, pitted and diced
- 12 fresh basil leaves
- 8 ounces of mozzarella balls, better known as ciliegine
- 12 slices of prosciutto
- 1 cup of crushed feta cheese
- Balsamic glaze, for drizzling (recipe below)
- ¼ cup of balsamic vinegar
- ¼ cup of honey

INSTRUCTIONS:

First make the balsamic glaze:

In a small saucepan, combine balsamic vinegar and honey. Simmer until reduced by half, stirring occasionally, 15 minutes (the mixture should coat the back of a spoon). Let cool slightly.

Assemble skewers: Layer cantaloupe, basil, mozzarella, prosciutto, and a second piece of cantaloupe until you have about 12 skewers.

Drizzle skewers with balsamic glaze and serve immediately

My Famous Crock Pot Rotel Dip

INGREDIENTS:

- 1 pound of ground turkey or beef (I use turkey)
- 1/2 cup of onion
- 2 cans of Mild Rotel tomatoes
- 2 tablespoon of olive oil
- 16 ounces of Velveeta cheese diced into blocks
- 3 tablespoons of my homemade taco seasoning
- 1 15-ounce container of salsa con queso
- 1 cup of milk
- 1 bag of tortilla chips or Doritos

Taco Seasoning Recipe:

- 1 tablespoon of chili powder
- ¼ teaspoon of garlic powder
- ¼ teaspoon of onion powder
- ¼ teaspoon of crushed red pepper flakes
- ¼ teaspoon of dried oregano
- ½ teaspoon of paprika
- 1 teaspoon of ground cumin
- ½ to 1 teaspoon of sea salt (more or less to taste)
- 1 teaspoon of black pepper

INSTRUCTIONS:

Set crockpot on high and add cans of Rotel and salsa con queso.

Take your ground turkey or beef and season with two table-spoons of taco seasoning.

Warm a frying pan with the 2 tablespoons of olive oil and add diced onions, once the onions start to brown add them to the crockpot.

Return pan back on stove top and on medium heat add the ground beef or turkey, once it browns add in blocks of Velveeta cheese, milk, and the remaining tablespoon of taco seasoning.

Once it starts to melt, add the mixture to the crockpot.

Sir the crock pot and let everything merry for 20 minutes on high.

Once everything marries and cooks, please serve with tortilla chips or Doritos.

* * *

SALAD RECIPES

WINTER

Roasted Vegetable Winter Dijon Vinaigrette Salad (Inspired by one of my favorite warm bowls from Sweet Green)

INGREDIENTS:

- 1 large sweet potato, peeled and diced
- 2 beets, quartered
- 1 pack of Brussels sprouts, cleaned and cut in half
- 3 tablespoons olive oil
- ½ cup pomegranate arils
- ½ cup pecans toasted
- 4 ounces goat cheese
- 8 cups kale or arugula
- 1 cup of cooked quinoa
- salt and fresh black pepper to taste

Dijon Vinaigrette:

- ¼ cup cider vinegar
- 3 tablespoons maple syrup
- 2 tablespoons Dijon mustard
- ¼ teaspoon garlic powder
- ½ cup extra virgin olive oil
- salt and fresh black pepper

INSTRUCTIONS:

Preheat oven to 425 F.

Toss sweet potatoes and Brussels sprouts with 2 tablespoons olive oil with salt and pepper and place on baking sheet. Toss beets with remaining olive oil and place on pan.

Season sweet potatoes and beets with salt and pepper. Roast 35-40 minutes or until tender. Remove from the oven and cool. Rub the skin of the beets to remove.

Combine all dressing ingredients in a small jar and shake well.

Add salad ingredients to a large bowl, including cooled beets, Brussels sprouts, and sweet potatoes. Drizzle with dressing and serve.

SPRING

Spring Salad with Strawberries, Watermelon Radishes, and Goat Cheese

---

INGREDIENTS:

- 4 cups of spring mix salad mix or romaine lettuce
- 1 ½ cup of strawberries, sliced
- 1 medium cucumber, seeded and sliced
- 1 large or 2 medium watermelon radishes, trimmed
- 6 ounces of honey or regular goat cheese, softened and crumbled (I prefer honey with this recipe)

- ¼ cup walnut pieces, can use slivered almonds or chopped pecans instead
- 1 cup Dijon vinaigrette (recipe below)

Dijon vinaigrette:

- ¼ cup apple cider vinegar
- ½ cup olive oil
- ¼ cup Dijon mustard
- 1 clove garlic, minced - you can also substitute it for 1 teaspoon garlic powder
- 1 teaspoon sea salt, add more if needed, to taste
- 1 teaspoon pepper, to taste

INSTRUCTIONS:

To a serving bowl, add all ingredients, except dressing. Toss to combine. When ready to serve, you can either add vinaigrette to bowl, or set aside for guests to dress themselves.

Dijon vinaigrette: Combine all ingredients to a mason jar. Secure lid and shake well to combine. Alternatively, you can also blend all ingredients together until dressing is thick and creamy, about 1-2 minutes.

Grilled Peach, Arugula, Goat Cheese, and Balsamic Vinaigrette Salad with a twist

---

INGREDIENTS:

- ¼ cup balsamic vinegar
- 2 tablespoons honey
- 3 tablespoons of fig jam
- 3 yellow peaches, pitted and each cut into 6 wedges (I prefer Georgia peaches)
- Cooking spray
- 1 tablespoon of extra virgin olive oil
- 1/8 teaspoon of freshly ground black pepper
- Dash of kosher salt
- 10 cups of trimmed arugula (about 10 ounces)
- 1 stalk of fennel, shaved
- 1 tablespoon of fresh chopped shallots
- 2 tablespoons crumbled goat cheese
- a handful of slivered almonds
- 1 pound of love

INSTRUCTIONS:

Bring vinegar to a boil in a small saucepan over medium-high heat. Reduce heat, and simmer until vinegar is reduced to 2 tablespoons (about 2 minutes). Remove from heat; stir in honey and fig jam. Cool to room temperature.

Prepare grill to high heat.

Place peach wedges on grill rack coated with cooking spray; grill 30 seconds on each side or until grill marks appear but peaches are still firm. Remove from grill; set aside.

Combine oil, pepper, and salt in a large bowl, stirring with a whisk. Add arugula and shallots, tossing gently with love to coat. Arrange arugula and fennel mixture on a platter. Top with peach wedges. Drizzle with balsamic vinaigrette; sprinkle with goat cheese crumbles and almonds

FALL

Apple Brussels Sprout Fall Salad

INGREDIENTS:
- 1 ½ pounds Brussels sprouts
- 1 cup of apples, diced
- ½ cup of feta cheese crumbles
- ½ cup of pecans, roughly chopped
- ½ cup of blueberries
- ½ cup of turkey or pork bacon, cooked and crumbled

For the dressing:

- 1 tablespoon of shallot, minced
- 1 teaspoon of garlic, minced
- 1/3 cup of olive oil
- 2 tablespoons of red wine vinegar
- 2 teaspoons of Creole or Dijon mustard
- 2 teaspoons of honey

- salt and pepper to taste

INSTRUCTIONS:

Cut the ends of the Brussels sprouts then cut them in half lengthwise. Thinly slice each Brussels sprout crosswise to cut into shreds.

Place the shredded Brussels sprouts in a bowl along with the apple, feta cheese, pecans, blueberries and bacon.

Place the shallot, olive oil, red wine vinegar, mustard, honey and salt and pepper in a jar. Shake to combine.

Pour the dressing over the salad. Toss to combine, then serve.

* * *

ENTREES

WINTER

Pot Roast

INGREDIENTS:

- 3 pounds of boneless chuck roast
- 4 10.5-ounce cans soup, beef broth or stock (broth makes a better au jus)
- 1 cup of water
- 1 white onion, cut into wedges

- 5 cloves of garlic, whole
- 1 16-ounce package carrots, sliced in two
- 1 bunch of fresh rosemary
- Salt
- Pepper
- Epis (herbs and spices)

INSTRUCTIONS:

Remember my epis recipe from chapter 4? Well, season chuck roast with epis, salt, and black pepper; sear in a large, deep skillet or Dutch oven over medium heat until browned, about 10 minutes per side.

Pour beef broth and water into the skillet with roast. Arrange onion wedges and garlic cloves around the meat. Spread carrots around the top of the roast and place sprig of rosemary on top of carrots. Turn heat to medium low and simmer until tender, about 6 hours. Please feel free to serve it with the Rosemary Garlic Mashed Potatoes (recipe below).

SPRING

Garlic Lemon Salmon, Broccolini, and Creamy Sweet Pea Pesto Zucchini and Spaghetti Noodles

---

INGREDIENTS:

- 1 serving of spaghetti
- 1 zucchini spiralized
- 3 tablespoons of my sweet pea pesto (see recipe below)

- 1 cup of heavy cream
- ¼ cup of milk
- ¼ cup of water
- 2 teaspoons of garlic powder
- 3 teaspoons of butter
- 1 teaspoon of salt
- ½ cup of parmesan cheese, shredded
- 1 pound of love

Sweet Pea Pesto

INGREDIENTS:

- 1 ¼ cup of frozen peas
- 1 clove garlic, peeled
- Salt and pepper to taste
- 1 teaspoon lemon juice
- ½ cup extra virgin olive oil
- 2 bunches of basil
- A few arugula leaves

Garlic Lemon Salmon and Broccolini

INGREDIENTS:

- 1 tablespoon of minced garlic
- 1 lemon sliced in three
- 16 ounces of salmon, cut in three
- 1 tablespoon of olive oil
- 4 tablespoons of salted butter

- 2 tablespoons of your preference of complete seasonings
- 1/3 cup of fresh chopped parsley
- 1 pound of love

INSTRUCTIONS:
Sweet Pea Pesto Zucchini and Spaghetti Noodles

Pesto:

In a medium skillet, heat 1 tablespoon of olive oil to medium. Add minced garlic and sauté for 3 minutes, until aromatic and golden brown.

Add basil, arugula, frozen peas, olive oil, lemon juice, salt, and pepper to food processor. Spoon the sautéed garlic into the processor as well, leaving the oil in the skillet.

Set the skillet aside for later.

Pulse the food processor until the pesto is well combined and mostly smooth. This will probably require some work, pausing occasionally to scrape down the sides in order to help to food processor do its job. If the pesto seems dry, add a bit more olive oil or lemon juice.

Spaghetti Noodles:

Bring a few inches of water, and a generous pinch of salt, to a boil in a saucepan.

Once the water is boiling, grab a handful of long noodles about the diameter of a quarter (about 1-inch) and add it to the pot. Cook the pasta until it is flexible, but not all the way to al dente.

Zucchini Noodles:

Spiralize your zucchini.

Depending on how you want to serve the dish, add zoodles to a large bowl and pour the sauce over top, mixing with tongs. Or serve zoodles in individual bowls and top with as much sauce as desired.

Sauce:

Heat heavy whipping cream, milk and water in a small, heavy saucepan over medium heat until hot but not boiling.

Add butter, pesto sauce, garlic powder and salt. Reduce heat and continue to cook about 5 more minutes over low heat.

Stir in ½ cup parmesan cheese until melted.

Allow the sauce to cool for 3 to 5 minutes before adding to zucchini and spaghetti noodles

Garlic Lemon Salmon and Broccolini

Preheat the oven to 400 F. Coat a baking sheet with nonstick spray. Arrange the salmon fillets in the center of the sheet.

In a small bowl with a fork, combine the butter, garlic, lemon zest, 2 tablespoons chopped fresh parsley, and black pepper. Mash to create a paste, then rub on the salmon fillets. If desired, arrange extra lemon slices on top.

Place the broccolini in a bowl. Drizzle with olive oil and sprinkle with your complete seasoning, salt, and black pepper. Toss to coat, then arrange around the salmon. Drizzle the lemon juice over the top of the salmon and broccolini.

Place the sheet pan in the oven and cook until the fish flakes easily with a fork for about 15 to 20 minutes.

Remove it and let it rest for a few minutes. Sprinkle with remaining parsley, then pare it with the pasta. Enjoy

SUMMER

Grilled Honey Harissa Chicken Kabobs

INGREDIENTS:

- 1 pound of boneless, skinless chicken breasts, cleaned with lime and cut into 1-inch pieces
- ¼ cup of olive oil
- 2 tablespoons of harissa paste
- ¼ cup of honey
- 1 teaspoon of minced garlic or 2 teaspoons of garlic powder
- Salt and pepper to taste
- 1 red bell pepper cut into 1-inch pieces

- 1 yellow bell pepper cut into 1-inch pieces
- 2 small zucchini cut into 1-inch slices
- 1 red onion cut into 1-inch pieces
- 1 pack of portobello mushrooms (optional)

INSTRUCTIONS:

Place the olive oil, harissa paste, honey, garlic and salt and pepper in a large bowl.

Whisk to combine.

Add the chicken, bell peppers, zucchini red onion, and mushrooms to the bowl, toss to coat in the marinade.

Cover and refrigerate for at least 1 hour, or up to 8 hours.

Soak wooden skewers in cold water for at least 30 minutes. Preheat grill or grill pan to medium high heat.

Fire up your grill.

Thread the chicken and vegetables onto the skewers.

Cook for 5-7 minutes on each side or until chicken is cooked through.

Coat with a little drizzle of honey and serve with the Grilled Peach Summer Salad.

Orange Sage Chicken

INGREDIENTS:

- 1 whole chicken
- 2 oranges
- 4 bunches of sage
- 2 tablespoons of Herb de Provence
- 1 tablespoon of orange-blossom honey
- Salt and pepper
- Gravy or au jus
- 1 tablespoon cornstarch
- ¼ cup water
- ¼ cup dry white wine or vermouth
- 1 pound of love
- Twine

INSTRUCTIONS:

Brine in ½ cup of apple cider vinegar, ½ cup of white vinegar, ½ cup of freshly squeezed orange juice, sage, salt, and 1 tablespoon of Herbs de Provence for 6-10 hours.

Once the chicken brines, coat with orange-blossom honey and place your whole chicken with the breast side up in an oven-safe skillet or roasting pan.

Preheat your oven at 375 F.

Roast your chicken for 20 minutes per pound, in my case 1 hour and 30 minutes.

Remove chicken from oven and reserve the pan drippings to make gravy or au jus.

Remove the chicken from the oven and let rest for 10 minutes in the pan. After the chicken has cooled, remove to a cutting board and let rest for an additional 10 minutes before carving (reserve the pan drippings in the pan to make your gravy).

While the chicken is cooling on the cutting board, defat your pan drippings by skimming the top with a spoon and reserving only the solids in the pan. Place your pan on your stove burner over medium-high heat, add ¼ cup white wine or vermouth. Reduce this mixture by about half.

Combine the cornstarch and water in a small mason jar or Tupperware and shake well to combine. Add this mixture to your reduced drippings and heat until the gravy has thickened. Serve over your carved chicken and pair with squash casserole and roasted asparagus.

***

SIDES

WINTER

Rosemary Garlic Mashed Potatoes

INGREDIENTS:
Rosemary-infused Garlic Confit:

- 8 cloves of garlic, peeled
- ¾ cup olive oil
- 2 bunches of fresh rosemary

Mashed Potatoes:

- 12 to 13 medium Yukon Gold potatoes (about 3 ½ pounds)
- 1 cup of half-and-half
- ½ cup of heavy whipping cream
- 4 ounces of Philadelphia cream cheese
- 8 tablespoons (1 stick) unsalted butter
- ½ teaspoon of black or white pepper
- Kosher salt

INSTRUCTIONS:

For the rosemary infused garlic confit: In a small saucepan over medium-low heat, simmer the garlic cloves in the oil for 15 to 20 minutes, in the last 5 to10 minutes, add the two bunches of rosemary. Then, let it cool. (Feel free to store in an airtight container, it will hold in the refrigerator for up to 2 weeks.)

For the mashed potatoes: Scrub and wash the potatoes and gently use a knife to go around the potato (this will help when peeling it), then place in a large stockpot and add cold water to cover. Season the water with a few tablespoons salt and bring to a boil. Cook until the potatoes are easily pierced with a fork, 25 to 30 minutes. Drain, and let cool for 2 to 4 minutes. Gently peel off the skins and transfer the potatoes back to stockpot.

In a small saucepan over low heat, warm the half-and-half, heavy whipping cream, cream cheese, and butter just until the butter is melted, about 2 minutes.

Add the half-and-half mixture and 8 cloves of the rosemary infused garlic confit and a few rosemary needles to the potatoes. Using a potato masher, mash until creamy. Season with the as much or as little of black or white pepper and salt that you need.

SPRING

Roasted Carrots

INGREDIENTS:
- 2 pounds carrots, peeled and sliced on diagonal
- 2 tablespoons of grapeseed oil or olive oil

- ½ teaspoon of salt (I typically use pink Himalayan salt)
- ¼ teaspoon of freshly cracked black pepper
- ½ teaspoon of paprika
- ½ teaspoon of garlic powder
- 2 tablespoons finely chopped fresh flat leaf or Italian parsley
- 1 tablespoon of chili powder
- ½ teaspoon ground cinnamon

INSTRUCTIONS:

Preheat the oven to 425 F.

Peel all the carrots and cut off the tops. Slice carrots on the diagonal so each piece is about

½-inch thick at the widest part. Each diagonal cut you make should be about 1 inch apart.

Add cut carrots to a LARGE sheet pan. Add olive oil, salt, pepper, paprika, chili powder, garlic powder, and cinnamon. Toss to coat all the carrots.

Spread carrots into one even layer and roast in the oven for 10 minutes. Remove from the oven and quickly toss/flip the carrots then return to the oven. Bake for another 8 to 15 minutes, until caramelized and tender. The roasting time may vary based on actual oven temperature, how spread out carrots are, and your personal preference for how roasted you want the carrots.

Remove the carrots from the oven. toss with fresh parsley and serve immediately.

SUMMER

Easy Roasted Asparagus

INGREDIENTS:

- 2 packs of asparagus from your local farmers market
- 1 red onion, sliced
- 1 shallot, sliced
- 3 tablespoons of your favorite seasoning mixture
- 1 teaspoon of garlic powder
- 1/3 of a cup of grapeseed oil or olive oil
- Himalayan Pink Salt
- Fresh ground black pepper
- 1 lemon wedge (optional)

INSTRUCTIONS:

Preheat your oven to 400 F.

Place asparagus, sliced shallots, and sliced red onion, on a rimmed baking sheet and drizzle with grapeseed oil or olive oil and season with your favorite seasoning mixture, garlic powder, salt, and pepper.

Use your hands to toss the asparagus, in the oil and seasonings and then arrange asparagus on the baking rack so they are not touching one and other.

Pop them into the oven for 20 minutes or until perfectly cooked.

Feel free to add a splash of fresh lemon juice on top, let it cool, and enjoy!

FALL

Squash Casserole (Inspired by my Aunt Janice)

INGREDIENTS:

- 2 medium yellow summer squash (about 2 cups, cooked, drained, and mashed)
- Trader Joe's Vegan Chickenless Seasoning Salt, add as much or less as you like
- Freshly ground black pepper, add as much or less as you like
- 1 Vidalia sweet onion, finely chopped
- ½ cup mayonnaise
- 1 large egg
- 1 teaspoon of sugar
- 1 teaspoon of garlic powder
- 4 tablespoons melted butter (divided)
- ¾ cup shredded sharp or mild cheddar cheese (divided)
- 1 cup of crushed Ritz crackers
- Salt
- 1 pound of love

INSTRUCTIONS:

Heat the oven to 350 F. Butter a 1-quart casserole or baking dish.

Slice or dice the summer squash and place it in a medium saucepan. Cover the squash with water and add 1 teaspoon of salt. Place the pan over high heat and bring the squash to a boil. Reduce the heat to medium-low and cover the pan; continue to cook until tender, or for about 10 to 15 minutes.

Meanwhile, peel the onion and cut it into halves; chop it finely.

Drain the squash thoroughly; return it to the saucepan and mash it with love. Taste the squash and add seasoning salt and pepper, as desired.

In a bowl, whisk the egg and sugar lightly. Add the mayonnaise, chopped onion, 2 tablespoons of the melted butter, and 1/2 cup of the cheddar cheese. Stir to blend thoroughly.

Mix the mashed squash into the egg and mayonnaise mixture, with love.

Spoon the mixture into the prepared casserole.

In a small bowl, using a fork mix the 1/4 cup of shredded cheese, breadcrumbs, and the remaining 2 tablespoons of melted butter and then sprinkle them over the casserole.

Bake for 30 minutes, or until bubbly and lightly browned.

* * *

DESSERTS

WINTER

Cranberry White Chocolate Sugar Cookies

INGREDIENTS:
- 1 cup butter softened, but not melted
- 1 ½ cups granulated sugar
- 1 large egg
- 1 teaspoon vanilla extract
- 2 ¾ cups all-purpose flour
- 1 teaspoon baking soda
- ½ teaspoon baking powder
- 3-4 tablespoons buttermilk, divided
- 1 cup of dried cranberries
- 1 bag of white chocolate morsels

INSTRUCTIONS:
Preheat oven to 375 F.

In a large mixing bowl, cream together butter and sugar until smooth.

Beat in the egg and vanilla. Set aside.

In a small bowl melt 1/3 of a cup of the white chocolate morsels.

In another small bowl, stir together flour, baking soda, and baking powder.

Gradually blend the dry ingredients into the wet ingredients.

Add just enough of the buttermilk to moisten the dough and make it soft, but not wet. (About a tablespoon or so).

Then mix in dried cranberries.

Afterwards roll dough into 1-inch balls or use a cookie scooper and place on an ungreased cookie sheet.

Bake for 8–9 minutes. Let stand for 2 minutes on the baking sheets before removing to cool on a rack.

In a separate bowl, melt the remaining white chocolate morsels

Once cookies cool dip, half of the cookie in the melted white chocolate and place on cooling rack

Feel free to then wrap the cookies in individual giveaway holiday goodie bags or store in an airtight container

---

Strawberry Key Lime Trifle (Inspired by Sarah Cook from Twelve Tomatoes)

INGREDIENTS:

- 1 box of strawberry cake mix + ingredients required on box
- 16 ounces of cream cheese, softened (about two boxes of Philadelphia Cream Cheese)
- ½ cup of powdered sugar
- ¼ cup of fresh lime juice (about 2 limes)
- 1 8-ounce container frozen whipped topping, thawed
- 6 cups strawberries, hulled and sliced
- 6 whole strawberries, for garnish
- Zest of 1 lime

INSTRUCTIONS:

Prepare 9x13-inch strawberry cake according to package instructions. Cool completely then cut into 1-inch cubes.

Beat cream cheese and sugar in a large mixing bowl until smooth and creamy. Add lime juice and beat until incorporated. Gently fold in thawed whipped topping.

To assemble, layer half of the cake cubes in the bottom of a trifle dish. Top with half of the cream cheese mixture and half of the sliced strawberries. Repeat layers ending with cream cheese mixture. Garnish with whole strawberries and lime zest.

My Southern Strawberry Fruit Punch Bowl Cake (Cheater Recipe)

INGREDIENTS:

- 1 box of French vanilla cake or angel food cake + ingredients required on the box
- 1 can of crushed pineapple, drained
- 2 pints fresh of strawberries, sliced
- 2 packages of vanilla instant pudding mix
- 3 cups of milk
- 2 8-ounce containers of Cool Whip
- 2 cans of Reddi-Wip
- 1 12-ounce can of maraschino cherries in light syrup, diced (optional)

INSTRUCTIONS:

Prepare French vanilla or angel food cake mix as directed on package. Bake on cookie sheet or 8x8-inch pan.

Let cake cool. Tear into small pieces.

Mix 2 packages vanilla pudding mix with 3 cups milk . Let this mixture set 30 minutes. Fold in one of 8 ounces containers Cool Whip.

While the mixture sets, dice your strawberries and a couple of cherries (optional), drain your pineapples

Remove the mixture from the refrigerator.

Then begin layering ingredients in punch bowl starting with cake, then strawberries, then pineapple, then cherries.

Next pour some of the pudding mixture over layers.

Next add a layer of Reddi-Wip over the layers.

Continue layering using the order just given until punch bowl is full. I like to top my final layer with Reddi-wip and strawberries to make it look cute

Refrigerate until ready to eat.

This makes a very large cake and is best when prepared the day before serving.

If you are in a time crunch, you can skip the last layer of Cool Whip and it is still wonderful.

FALL

Homemade Pumpkin Brownies

INGREDIENTS:
Brownie Layer

- 1 cup of all-purpose flour
- 1 cup of brown sugar

- 1 cup of unsweetened cocoa powder
- 1 ¼ cups of white sugar
- 4 eggs
- 1 stick of salted butter, save some butter for the pan
- 2 tablespoons of vegetable oil
- 1 bag of semisweet chocolate chips or chunks (I prefer chunks)
- 1 ½ tablespoon of vanilla extract
- 1 teaspoon of sea salt
- 1 pound of love through whisking and folding

Pumpkin Layer

- 1 8-ounce block cream cheese, softened
- 1 cup pumpkin puree
- ¾ cup sugar
- 1/3 teaspoon of pumpkin spice
- 1 tablespoon vanilla extract
- ¼ cup heavy cream
- 2 large eggs lightly beaten

INSTRUCTIONS:

Preheat oven to 375 F. Butter a 13x9-inch pan and set it aside.

In a microwave safe bowl, add the butter. Heat in the microwave on HIGH for about 30 - 45 seconds. Remove, stir, and cool on the counter for 5 minutes, then stir in the vanilla extract and cocoa powder.

In the bowl of a stand mixer add the warm (but not hot) butter/cocoa mixture, pumpkin puree and vegetable oil.

With mixing speed on low add one egg at a time, mixing just until incorporated.

In a medium size mixing bowl, whisk together brown sugar, flour, salt, and white sugar. With mixing speed on low, gradually add dry ingredients. Mix until no flour pockets remain. Remove bowl from stand and fold in the chocolate chips or chunks with the vanilla extract. (Save some chocolate chips or chunks for the next step

Make the pumpkin layer by beating the cream cheese in an electric mixer until it's smooth and creamy. Beat in the rest of the ingredients until you have a smooth pumpkin batter and no lumps remain.

Top the brownie batter in the dish with the pumpkin batter. Drop the rest of the brownie batter into the pumpkin batter, using a knife or skewer to swirl it together.

Bake the brownies for 40 to 45 minutes, or until a toothpick inserted in the center comes out clean. Let cool completely before cutting and serving!

* * *

COCKTAILS

WINTER

Cranberry Fizz Cocktail (Inspired by Jordyn, Almost Supermom)

INGREDIENTS:

- 2 tablespoon of leftover orange-cranberry sauce
- 2 ounces gin
- 2 ounces Cointreau
- Ice
- Club soda
- Fresh rosemary for garnish

INSTRUCTIONS:

Combine cranberry sauce, gin, Cointreau, and ice into a martini shaker.

Shake vigorously for 15 seconds.

Fill tumbler glass with ice.

Pour cranberry mixture over ice.

Fill the rest of the glass with club soda.

Garnish with fresh rosemary and cranberries.

*To make this a mocktail, replace gin and Cointreau with orange juice.

Pink Grapefruit Cocktail

INGREDIENTS:

- 4 ounces fresh pink grapefruit juice, plus grapefruit wedge for garnish
- ½ ounce fresh lemon juice
- ½ ounce of Triple Sec
- 2 ounces of Ruby Red vodka
- Coarse brown sugar (optional garnish)
- 2 tablespoons of simple syrup, for sweetness (optional)

INSTRUCTIONS:

To garnish the glass, wet the rim of a chilled martini glass with a little of the grapefruit juice and then dip the rim into the brown sugar and add grapefruit edge.

Shake the grapefruit and lemon juice, triple sec, vodka, simple syrup (optional) and 1 tablespoon crushed ice in a cocktail shaker. Add a touch more fruit juice or vodka to taste. Strain into the martini glass. Enjoy!

Strawberry Rose Petal Margaritas (Inspired by Cassie Winslow, Deco Tartelette)

INGREDIENTS:
- ¼ cup of fresh strawberries, chopped fine
- ¼ cup of fresh lime juice (2 limes)
- 1 tablespoon of fresh lemon juice (½ a lemon)
- 3 tablespoons of rose petal simple syrup (recipe below)
- 4 ounces of tequila
- 1 ounce of Chambord
- Handful of ice (If you love the flavor of rose petals as much as I, freeze a tray of rose water and add a few to the ice mix)
- Salt or sugar to rim each glass
- Fresh strawberries slices for garnish

INSTRUCTIONS:
First, make the rose petal simple syrup (recipe below).

Place strawberries, lime juice, lemon juice, and rose petal simple syrup in a large bowl. Using an immersion blender, blend the mixture for about 10 seconds or so (you can also use a blender). Then, add tequila and Chambord. Rim two mason jars of your choice with salt or sugar and fill with ice. Divide the mixture between two jars. Garnish with fresh strawberry slices.

Rose Petal Simple Syrup

INGREDIENTS:

- 2 cups of sugar
- 1 cup of water
- ¼ cup of edible dried rose petals (If you don't have a farmers market nearby, look for edible flowers in the produce or tea section (not the florist section!) of your local grocery store)

INSTRUCTIONS:

Place all ingredients in a pot over the stove and bring to a boil.

Then reduce heat so the mixture is simmering.

Simmer for 5 minutes or until the mixture has reduced to a syrup.

Let cool, then strain into a bowl through a fine mesh sieve.

Store in the fridge in a clean glass bottle or mason jar.

It should last for approximately one week. I normally add it to my summer iced lattes throughout the week.

Blood Orange Bourbon Sour Cocktail (Inspired by Danielle Esposti, Our Salty Kitchen)

INGREDIENTS:

- 1 ¼ ounces of blood orange juice, plus orange slices for garnish
- 2 ¼ ounces of bourbon
- 1 ounce of simple syrup (Recipe Below)
- 1 ounce of lemon juice
- ½ ounce of lime juice
- 2 maraschino cherries for garnish

INSTRUCTIONS:

Roll a blood orange back and forth on a cutting board a few times to break up the flesh and release the juices. Cut the orange in half, and juice using a reamer or the tines of fork.

Fill a cocktail shaker with ice. Pour 1 ounce blood orange juice, bourbon, simple syrup, lemon juice, and lime juice into the shaker. Stir until the shaker frosts.

Place 1 large ice cube into a cocktail glass.

Pour the blood orange cocktail into the glass and garnish with a blood orange slice and a maraschino cherry.

Simple Syrup

INGREDIENTS:

- 2 cups of sugar
- 1 cup of water

INSTRUCTIONS:

Combine the two cups of sugar and one cup of water in a small saucepan and heat over medium-high heat, whisking frequently until the sugar is dissolved and the solution is clear. Remove from heat and cool.

Then pour simple syrup in a mason jar; it should last for two months.

Throughout the various seasons, I hope you can use these recipes to entertain and host a few friends sometime soon.

9

IMPACT AN EXCHANGE

———

There's something about the worded doormats in front of someone's home that shares their sense of humor or acceptance into their home. I personally love the doormats that say, "Welcome," "Home Sweet Home," or "Be Our Guest, but not for too long because then it gets weird."

However, once you ring the doorbell or knock on the door, they sometimes either let you in with a hug or a big welcome to my or our home. This is then followed by offering you something to drink or water and often telling you to make yourself home. You then start to have some small talk that evolves into a conversation. At the same time, you take in both the conversation and the smell of the food prepared in the kitchen. Afterward, they invite you over to the table, and you break bread with that person while still sharing stories or having a meaningful conversation. This often comes to an end with a dessert, some leftovers to take home, thank yous and goodbyes.

That night you then leave with a memory, an unforgettable time, stories, sometimes delicious food, and the experience of feeling welcomed. The "they" in this scenario is me. I love hosting family, friends, or new friends because of the opportunity to do the following:

- Invite someone over
- Make them feel welcomed
- Eat great food
- Have great conversations
- Gain the fulfillment of having company over to have a good time

It leaves me with a memory that will last forever and, depending on the relationship, countless stories to tell in the future. I can bet my last dollar that anyone I've hosted can say that they too were grateful to catch up and eat some fantastic food. In the end, I think my family, friends, or guests can agree that the exchange of them coming over and being entertained and leaving feeling welcome are things to be thankful for, because it deepens our relationships with one another. I'm glad that in chapter 9, I shared all of those great recipes because, in this chapter, I will share how we can take those delicious dishes to create some extraordinary exchanges.

GRUBS AND GRATITUDE

We can all agree that it's often been nice to feel heard, seen, or welcomed when going to pre-COVID social networks, a friend's BBQ, happy hours, and other social gatherings. Sometimes at the social networking events or happy hours, the venue or bar provides us with bar height tables in different room areas with limited sitting that forces even the introverts to engage. We then indulge in the appetizers and sip on our drinks as we talk business, give an elevator pitch about ourselves, and exchange business cards. The great exchanges of the happy hour are that we often follow up these happy-hour engagements by:

- Adding the people you met to LinkedIn
- Reaching out to meet up with that person later to grab coffee or lunch
- Utilizing those opportunities to build on that relationship

The benefits of these exchanges would be that sometimes, that person becomes a future mentor, friend, colleague, reference, potential business partner, or another person that we know in town.

However, at a friend's BBQ, depending on where you live, the setup is different. Still, the benefits of the exchange remain the same. It may take place in their backyard near a pool, on a balcony at their apartment or condo, or on their patio. You then have different stations to top your burger, grab a drink, help yourself to some sides, and find the desserts. There are often seating areas during the BBQ. Everyone is standing around, talking, and attempting to catch up or meet someone's new partner, friend, dog, or kids. You may make a new friend based on similar interests or desire to have that person in your circle. You rarely leave a happy hour, social network, or BBQ without a shared drink, appetizer, meal, and or a conversation with someone old or new, and that is where your greatest exchange begins to happen.

When you think about it, the word *exchange* means "the act of giving or taking one thing in return for another."[68] During an exchange, someone is then thankful or welcomed, but both persons can feel a sense of gratitude at the end of the exchange. I understand that there aren't happy stories at the end of every interaction. The term exchange may have a selfish connotation. I'd like to look at the flip side. Like the wins in our relationships, community, and networks, each time we exchange a meal or drink with someone. For we deepen our connections with one another every time. I've shared my story of when I first moved to DC and how my community and various meal exchanges and conversations turned a strange place into a home for me. Now, I understand that every encounter or relationship will not make a place home, but it will have a communal feel. I think that part of feeling welcome holds our relationships together, whether it's a professional or personal relationship. When you feel welcomed, you share stories, insights, jokes, pastimes, strategies, or resourceful information because you're in a space where it's been said or unsaid that it's okay to be you due to the support, appreciation, or the feelings of being valued. We have all been the new kid around the block at some point in our lives. We live in a cold world, but what makes it warm are the chances that we get to being welcomed into a building, someone's life, an opportunity.

---

68 *Merriam-Webster.com Dictionary*, s.v. "exchange, (n.)," accessed October 3, 2020.

BACKYARD DIPLOMATIC BITES

During my book writing journey, I got the chance to interview writer, journalist, and community diplomacy expert Maria de los Angeles. I asked her how did she successfully bring people together and build community through her connection efforts. She shared she learned how to do this through a freelance opportunity with Global Ties Miami. She helped a Nigerian doctors' delegation with the Zika crisis. She said:

> *Global Ties Miami was co-hosting them as they were here with the CDC studying epidemics. As an ordinary citizen, I was protesting very evolvable happening with Zika, and it was. In that effort that the Director of Global Ties got to know me. I then got the chance to talk with these doctors privately. I would help with their dogs, babies, and families and share meals with them. I thought that it was just fantastic because I have never done that before. I'm a journalist, a writer, and so on. Still, I've never thought that I could just sit down with people internationally like that. As a citizen, I have a role in diplomacy and mutual understanding. It was an amazing experience. I gleaned a lot from them, and they learned a lot from me, and then I was able to share that conversation with people.*

So, she then moved to DC after being her parent's caretaker in Miami and continued to freelance for Global Ties Miami with their fellowship program. When she moved into her studio apartment in DC, she decided that she would host one of these dinners because that's what they did in Miami. Maria then shared with me that after having this experience with the Nigerian doctors, she was also very excited about delegating another particular cohort's delegation because they were all women from Latin America. So, Maria had them over at her little studio in a tiny little place. They were excited to meet her, she prepared a DC sampler, and they had a fantastic evening. Her biggest takeaways were the heartfelt conversations about what it's like to be a woman in their countries and their fields of work and their effort to be leaders in their field. Maria shared:

> I'll never forget it. It was incredible, and it was amazing that an average person can do this, and that kind of start to make a difference. I have a doctoral-level education, but nothing replaces the experience of the person-to-person contact and breaking bread, and then actually talking about what life is like every day. In that case, it was Venezuela, Guatemala, and Mexico, face to face. We cried, laughed, and learned things that I would never learn just from reading a newspaper, of what life was really like for these women and what they were doing, quietly. That time together turned into a sacred, safe space. We can turn our homes into embassies that welcome people, break bread with them, and learn their stories. No matter what we see in the news, or what happens in the high courts or in the international, in the UN or don't do, you can do this in your own backyard.

EATING AT OUR EMBASSIES

Maria is totally right; we can do this in our own backyards or homes. Also, if you think about it our homes are indeed embassies for family members, friends, and others. The term embassy means, "the official residence and offices of an ambassador."[69] The term ambassador means "an authorized representative or messenger."[70] So, if you think about it, we are all representatives of our own homes or "embassies." There's something special and impressive to guest or friends when hosting a dinner party. Inviting others into your home, preparing a meal for them to eat, and preparing a space for them to be and enjoy their evening changes you. As I've shared in previous chapters breaking bread with others has been a heavily respected and practiced tradition since the beginning of time. The plus side to it is that it's a fun and simple way to spend some time with old friends or make new friends through friends of friends. It's a way of silently telling a person that they are welcomed and accepted. So, I have created this nice list on how to turn our homes into embassies when hosting friends, family, or guest for dinner parties:

- Create a theme (this is not a must, but it makes decorations and food options easier to select)
- Send out invitations with some rules for the night (i.e., bring your appetite)
- Light some candles (scents can be based on season or theme; it also makes the house smell nice)

---

69 *Merriam-Webster.com Dictionary*, s.v. "embassy," accessed October 4, 2020.

70 *Merriam-Webster.com Dictionary*, s.v. "ambassador," accessed October 4, 2020.

- Set up the table and add a few decorations (don't forget to write down the Wi-Fi password)
- Have the food warm and ready to go about 15 minutes before your guests arrive (the warm setting on your oven is your best friend)
- Prepare cocktails and appetizers and offer them to your guest as you say hello
- Help them help themselves
- Start conversations near the food (i.e., ask who likes pomegranate in their hummus or touch on something a dish reminds you of; this will spark conversations)
- Enjoy the food
- Have your dessert either ready to share or packed up in a to-go bag
- Take photos to hold on to your memories

Also, just a disclaimer, if you don't feel like cooking the recipes that I have shared, you can turn this into a potluck event and pick up your favorite entree from your local restaurants and have everyone else bring sides to complement it. Personally, if I don't want to cook but still want to entertain or host friends, I have a theme like Chinese Take-out Night, and we watch movies like Freaky Friday to set the mood. Or, we might have an English Tea Brunch and have scones, tea, and things to set the mood. Of course, like I've shared above, once there is a mood or an ambiance that encourages conversation, people will start speaking and you'll have that palate and people experience.

HUMAN CONNECTION THROUGHOUT THE WORLD

One of Maria's other points that she brought up that I would like to focus on is the great exchanges in our world, and how we can experience a country through the stories that others share. I started thinking about how communities and business relationships are formed or how networks are built worldwide. Depending on where you are in the world, it may take several dinners, coffees, or teas for someone to gain your trust enough to start personal conversations. In other parts of the world it may take one coffee or lunch before someone unveils their personal stories or goals.

During my graduate program, I had the chance to take a Cultural Aspects of Global Engagement course. After leaving this course, my cohort and I left ready and eager to advocate and communicate on issues and commitments to diverse audiences and the general markets. Due to discussions, simulations, activities, and research that helped us understand multicultural communities and diverse institutions, customs, and traditions in means of both business and personally, we learned engagement strategies and techniques through several cross-cultural simulations and assignments. For one of our major simulation projects, we prepared our communications strategy for a prospective client or engagement through research and the help of Erin Myers, The Culture Map: Breaking Through the Invisible Boundaries of Global Business, Culture Map application. This map would take our home country (USA) and the country of the person or company we wish to engage with. This application gives us guidance and insights into their outlook on how to communicate and form relationships abroad. We would be encouraged to look at different world regions that piqued our interest in business relationships worldwide. I remember choosing to look at Latin America, Northern Africa, the Middle East, and Southeast Asian countries for fun due to previous or desired business travel, relationships, or vacation.

However, in my simulation report assignment, I remember focusing on how I would approach advocating for women's rights and higher education access for girls in mainland China. Now, going into this assignment, I thought it would be easy as pie because my undergraduate thesis covered the importance of women's rights and girls' access to higher education. But, in the course of creating this advocacy cultural strategy plan, I had to be mindful of cross-cultural differences and approach the situation without bringing offense. Which is different than just compiling research and building a defense. Fortunately, I traveled to China earlier that term for a global residency and was able to reach out to a few friends for advice on the best way to approach this advocating for this concept. They told me to be mindful of their values, approach it from the aspect of growth and its positive effects to their economies, and include a business dinner as part of my strategy plan.

Now, here in the US, business dinners and lunches are important as well. So, I realized that food can be used as soft power in business, advocacy approaches, or diplomatic relations, which I'll discuss more about in a future chapter. However, "personal relationships are important in any business context, but to build successful relationships in China it is crucial to start by understanding cultural differences. This is especially true in social situations like business lunches and dinners."[71] Our human connection has a positive effect in building relationships around us during a meal exchange and that is proven during both personal and business interactions. Needless to say, that in my report I mentioned the dinner and it being used as a soft power in the proposal realms of things along with other supported strategies and impacts and I aced my paper.

Imagine what our world would look like if we opened our homes or backyards to family, friends, and friends of friends and started small talk conversations that evolved into special moments. We would all be a part of something that makes a much larger impact. Also, if you're not inclined to opening up your home, you can always have dinner in your "backyard" at local restaurants. Thanks to your foodie friends on social media or yelp, you can easily find restaurants that accommodate you and your guest's dining preferences and there's lest clean up on your end. Either way, when our inspirations turn into initiatives, we can make an impact. Ultimately, it is a win, and each one of us can cause the greatest exchanges to happen in our society or world by adding an extra seat to the table or hosting a few guests.

71   Ting Zhang, "Doing Business with China: Business Dinner Etiquette," LinkedIn, August 2, 2018.

10

PLEASING PALATES, APPEASING PEOPLE

In international relations, sharing food with people from different cultures to break down barriers is called culinary diplomacy.[72]

—DANA AL MARASHI, HEAD OF CULTURAL
DIPLOMACY AT THE UAE EMBASSY

Have you heard of the cliche line "the best way to someone's heart is through their stomach?" Well, that statement stands true. Just as most of us use foods like ice cream, brownies, popcorn, pretzels, chips and dip, etc. to ease our edge or emotionally support our feelings, food has the effect to please both your palate and in a way temporarily pacify our situations. As I shared in previous chapters, food has the power to bring us together, or at least serve as a catalyst of

---

72 Rong Qin, "Diplomacy on the Dinner Table," *Diplomatic Courier,*
March 30, 2019.

bringing people together regardless of differences because we all must eat. Moreover, as I've also shared before, food is used as a tool to bring people together in business, our social avenues, and politics. While politics is always a hot button discussion and most try to dodge the conversation depending on the setting—food can be used as a mechanism of soft power to ease the tension. The political science definition of soft power is the ability of a country to persuade others to do what it wants without force or coercion.[73] Now in layman's terms, soft power just means the ability to persuade, attract, or influence a leader or a country to take a certain position on policy, or a particular stance on a situation, without taking extreme measures that may lead to tension, future conflict, division, or war.

Now unbeknownst to most, culinary diplomacy has the effect of soft power without it screaming too loud that it's the plan or agenda to resolve conflict. Culinary diplomacy, also known as gastrodiplomacy, is known to be the method of which the best way to win hearts and minds through the stomach. "Gastrodiplomacy, culinary diplomacy, and war gastronomy are terms used in different contexts and fields with a wide range of explanations to illustrate to what extent food could be impactful at promoting any country or community's gastronomic richness and diversity. Beyond the definition or usage of the term, it can be expanded to the humanitarian and development fields."[74] "Gastrodiplomacy,

---

73   Joseph S. Nye, "Soft Power: The Means to Success in World Politics," *Foreign Affairs Magazine*, May/June 2004.

74   Doğan Çelik, "The Healing Effect of Gastrodiplomacy in Conflict-Affected Communities," *Policy,* 2018.

[is] how countries conduct cultural diplomacy through promotion of their cuisine, it's an increasing popular strategy for public diplomacy and nation branding. [Gastrodiplomacy can be used as] a strategy of middle powers trying to create better brand recognition. Numerous middle powers have invested significant capital resources in culinary diplomacy projects to enhance global awareness of their respective cultures as a means to further nation brand status and soft power."[75]

Recently, the Meridian International Center and the Embassy of the United Arab Emirates (UAE) organized a lunch discussion around the concept of culinary diplomacy through sharing the diverse cuisines and the hospitable culture in UAE, especially in Abu Dhabi. One of the panelists was Ambassador Barbara Leaf, former U.S. Ambassador to the UAE (2014 to 2018). During the discussion, she shared the story of when she served as a Middle East specialist in Paris. The U.S. ambassador there called her in urgency and asked for a way to make people who did not usually talk to each other talk, especially with the American negotiators. She then booked the best Middle East restaurant in Paris. "The food completely changed the atmosphere in the room," she said, "food was a remarkable way to break the ice, especially for people who convene in a room in a foreign country and talk about difficult issues."[76] "Food is never just about the ingredients. It is embedded in a nation's history, culture, and

75   Paul S. Rockower, "Recipes for Gastrodiplomacy," *Place Branding and Public Diplomacy* 8, no. 3 (2012): 235-246.

76   Rong Qin, "Diplomacy on the Dinner Table," *Diplomatic Courier*, March 30, 2019.

people's lifestyles. In this way, sharing food with people connects them at fundamental levels and promotes deep understanding of a culture's values and traditions. Sometimes a dinner table can achieve more than what a negotiation table can."[77] In previous chapters, I've shared how food has played a role in our senses and how various aromas, aesthetics, and the food within itself can shift our judgement and outlook of a culture, but the standards apply the same when looking at settling our differences and resolving conflict.

CHEERS TO BUSINESS AND RELATIONSHIPS

The same mechanism of soft power applies in the business and lobbying world. Strong and stable relationships are vital for the success of not only friendships, but also businesses. I recently read a *Forbes* article on business and people, where Tina Hovsepian shares several reasons why companies who embrace the culture of building relationships with those who are within the business of which its success thrives on along with tips on maintaining relationships. Oftentimes, I think some people forget the amount of work it takes to build our relationships, that it takes twice as much work to maintain those relationships. According to Tina, there are four vital groups or relationships that every business and professional must invest in, which are your "vendors/consultants, employees, partners, and your clients, members, and customers."[78] While it's a given that you must do your best investing in those who invest in your business, the same

---

77 Ibid.

78 Tina Hovespian, "Business and People: Why Relationships are Essential for a Successful Business," *Forbes*, July 20, 2018.

applies to your employees who support your mission. Investing in your partners, who may bring in future partnerships and extending opportunities, along with vendors and consultants who supply products or services to your business, is necessary, too. Ways that you can go about that goes beyond communicating it in reviews, but also expressing appreciation tangibly. Maybe ice cream socials, catered company lunches, and other various company gatherings will help to spread the good news of the company's and partners' successes. While everyone would like a monetary raise or sort of gift, the personal touches of lunches, socials, and gatherings that allows the human connections parts of business leaders or businesses to be shown can not only shift the culture but also it will increase the amount of success that you build throughout the year.

I often think of why people remember the reason, aesthetics, or foods at an event much quicker than people who attend them sometimes. The reason why is because those events nine times out of ten had great menus or drinks, which drew out a memory. Think of times when you re-introduce yourself to someone if you didn't meet them at a professional setting, concert, or other common locations; you would've met them at a social engagement where food was involved. Remember when I said food is also a memory, well "the role of emotion in memory is complex. While positive emotions may improve recall, some stressful experiences are suppressed from memory."[79] Those positive moments influence our memories and

79   Nigel Barber, "Why Some People Remember Events Better than Others," *Psychology Today*, October 22, 2019.

allow smooth transitions into conversations when meeting someone again.

I remember taking an international lobbying course during my graduate program and the number one story that would be shared was how our professor (he's a former lobbyist), classmates who lobby, or guest speakers navigate the world of lobbying. One of the biggest takeaways from that course about how to navigate global advocacy through strategic lobbying plans, was the importance of building and maintaining our business relationships. The top stories that would be shared are the various dinner, lunch, or happy hour exchanges that would allow these relationships to be formed. This led me to ponder on how lobbyist use this same measure of "soft power" or "culinary diplomacy" to either gain access to policy makers or influence policy makers to shift their stance or compromise on supporting various policies or laws. While some may look at this as a bribe or an opportunity for public or private interest to try to sway government. I looked at this method as a strategy to please one's plate by compromising on either a solution or decision through appeasing one's plate through culinary diplomacy/gastrodiplomacy.

Friendships and relationships are what allows our society and businesses to thrive. Most businesses rise through word of mouth, recommendations, and reviews, and so thanks to the friends who may be stakeholders, respected in their community and networks, or influencers. We all need each other to get somewhere. So, what better way to keep our relationships going than sharing a meal, cookie and tea, coffee, or brunch?

IV

11

TAKING THE FINAL BITE

———

Food is maybe the only universal thing that really has the power to bring everyone together. No matter what culture, everywhere around the world, people get together to eat.

—GUY FIERI[80]

While everyone has their own truths, traditions, cultures, norms and customs, our common ground is food. We all have to pause and eat. When we do pause and take in the amazing meals that are in front of us, those moments become more special when we allow others to join us. The simple exchange of sharing a meal or breaking bread with others allows us to form friendships or other valuable relationships. Throughout the book, I touched on nine various topics of that prove how powerful palates are and the effects of when we encounter one of life's greatest exchanges when we share meals with others.

The nine topics or concepts that were shared were:

———

80   Guy Fieri, BrainyQuote.com, *BrainyMedia Inc*, 2020.

1. Understanding how we are able to connect through breaking bread and finding connection, understanding, and exchange with one another, and food mends everything together.
2. How food influences our motivations to travel or try new things, and the influence of various cultures in different dishes. Understanding what culture identity is and its influence on our desire of sharing various dishes.
3. The beauty of food, memory, and hospitality coming together.
4. The importance of being transparent and sharing your truth and traditions with others and allowing those moments to tear down the invisible boarders of various cultures and customs.
5. Understanding that there are no language barriers to our taste buds. We all are able to say *Mmm* to various dishes and are able to build community around that.
6. Understanding the history of food and peace.
7. The importance of allowing our palates to shift and understanding the reciprocal respect that happens during our dining experiences.
8. The importance of turning our homes into embassies and learning about each other.
9. Understanding the impact of an exchange and the changes that can be made.

The beauty of all of these concepts is that we win each other's hearts when we exchange or share a meal. Our palates are more powerful than we give credit to them and we begin to grow as people when we allow those delicate moments of human connection to happen. Now, I didn't write all of this to say that exchanging a meal will rid of every conflict or situation, but be mindful that the power that lies in your palate shifts not only your judgement, but also your influence. I want to share a few examples of how I am building and maintaining, meaningful relationships through gastrodiplomacy in hopes that you can see how powerful this movement really is.

* * *

NONPROFIT FUNDRAISING

One of my biggest advocacy points/passions/interest is women in leadership and educating girls. I would like to briefly take you through an exchange on how this would work with using food to help steer the conversation to promote educating girls in various countries.

For example, consider the nonprofit organization, She's the First (STF). This organization builds a community of advocates that range from policymakers and teachers, to parents that fights for a world where every girl chooses her own future. She's the First often teams up with twelve local organizations in eleven countries to make sure girls are educated, respected, and heard. She's the First currently needs support regarding their fundraising and advocacy mechanisms; therefore, I have created a plan using gastrodiplomacy to increase STF's support and advocacy outreach efforts.

Option 1: Improving Existing Efforts to Raise More Money

- My first recommendation would be for She's the First to continue their existing fundraising efforts but with a twist. The Bake a Change challenge, Cheese the First gatherings, and Do It Yourself are all excellent efforts for awareness and fundraising; however, if we turn these efforts into community events, more hearts can be touched, changed, and left wanting to partner with She's the First. This option is low-risk and cost efficient.

Option 2: Using She's the First's Global Impact to Make an Impact

- We noticed that She's the First is not only interested in changing the life of girls, but it also celebrates diversity. There is no better way to display diversity than through an international festival. This would be a great opportunity to have the girls from all twelve countries showcase their cultures and knowledge through food, art, and talent at different booths. This option worked perfectly for our last client; it was cost efficient and helped raise over $350,000 dollars at a five-hour festival.

Option 3: Creating an Annual Gala

- A gala would be an excellent opportunity for She's the First to raise money. The talent, world-renowned chefs, and speakers list can be a great tactic to inspire or convince individuals to purchase gala tickets. The prices of the tickets can be broken down into different packages so that the night can be even more spectacular. The package options at different prices could include one's ticket, an item (artwork, bracelet, or gift) designed by the girls, and other exclusive information and details about more opportunities to engage. Also, our social team would work diligently to promote and spread the word across all social media platforms including Facebook, Instagram, Twitter, and Tik-Tok.

RESULTS OF USING GASTRODIPLOMACY

The Unstoppable Foundation is an organization that is similar to She's the First in terms of expanding education. In 2017 they shared an article on the success of their Unstoppable Gala, "raising a total of $920,000. The Proctor Gallagher Institute started the evening by generously pledging to double their last year's financial support [totaling] $520,000 that will go toward the sustainability and expansion of the work of the Unstoppable Foundation. In addition, the attendees donated $400,000 of which 100 percent will go directly toward bringing an education and a future to 1,500 children in the Maasai Mara, Kenya, with our implementing partner, Free the Children. We had a sold-out house with over 550 people in attendance. ABC 7 News anchors David Ono and Ellen Leyva opened the evening as our media sponsor and Marilyn McCoo and Billy Davis Jr. brought the house down when they sang the invocation, "Amazing Grace." Honorary co-chairs Brandy and Malcolm-Jamal Warner did a fantastic job setting up the evening and our host, John Schneider, was not only fabulous but a little intimated by our unstoppable auctioneer, Karen Sorbo! There were exciting performances by the Australian Tenors ARIA, and violinist Elizabeth Bacher, as well as dramatic readings by Martin Sheen, Brandy and Shiza Shahid. Malala Yousafzai, the brave Pakistani girl who stood up to the Taliban for the right of girls to attend school, was the 2014 Unstoppable Achievement Award honoree. The award was presented to Shiza Shahid, CEO of the Malala Fund."[81]

COMMUNITY INVOLVEMENT IN CAMPAIGNING

Gastrodiplomacy can also be used when campaigning. Our political world would be different if our leaders were to allow everyone from different backgrounds, political stances, private sector, public sector, teachers, doctors, lawyers, pharmaceutical employees, healthcare workers, small business owners and more to sit at the table, dine, and exchange in conversation about what needs to change. It's not a kumbaya moment but a learning moment. You have a local restaurant cater the event and allow your representee to share their insights. The food breaks the tension, and the candidate is able to be a little bit more personable. We are stronger when we are together and united and what better way to make that happen by giving someone not only a seat but also the chance to raise their voice and appease their palates. After all, food doesn't only suppress our hunger or help up grow physically. We also grow mentally through our connections, for food is universal, food is friendship, and more. When we

---

81 Team Unstoppable, "Oh What a Night!" *Unstoppable Foundation*, March 19, 2017.

form lasting friendships, business relationships, or treaties, we build unity and help to keep the peace. There is Power in our Palates and our world changes through one of life's greatest exchanges—sharing a meal.

ACKNOWLEDGMENTS

Writing this book afforded me the opportunity to cross paths with everyday travelers, ambassadors, chefs, foodies, and dining connoisseurs. Each conversation gave me new insights and made this book a reality. Thank you to all of individuals for sharing your precious time and stories.

Soonhoon Ahn

Coren Allen

Nadia Aziz

Lauren Bernstein

Jason Butler

Marcus Cammack

Maria de Los Angeles

Jeremiah Devlin-Ruelle

Reina Gascon-Lopez

Manal Kahn

Amy Kolzack

Marie Lerch

Veaceslav Pituscan

Chad Sandhaus

Ted Sickley

Susan Sloan

George Stone

Niya Watkins

Jane Zimmerman

To my family, friends, family friends, mentors, and colleagues who made this book possible. Whether it was introducing me to your connections, praying with me, giving me pep-talks, editing chapters, providing moral support when writing or revising, simply being a part of the journey, or believing in my book's vision enough to support me—thank you.

A special note to my momma and sister, Kettelye Louisius and Mildred "Millie" LeJeune. Both of you have been there through every step of the way and I love you for it. Momma, my life and this book are possible because of you. Millie, your dedication and determination to do your own thing inspired me to share my passions with the world.

A special note for my late grandmother, Venita aka Grams, I promised you before you passed that I would do this, and your Kathi did it! You've taught me what it means to care for others and the importance of forming and keeping relationships through cooking and sharing meals. Your legacy will continue to live on through me and I hope to keep inspiring if not thousands than millions!

A special note to my roommates and friends Amanda Bryson, Rachel Bradley, Julia Nista, Reginald "Reggie" Clark, Michelle Risse, and Ted Sickley for helping me edit my chapters and expand on stories throughout my book writing journey.

To Eric Koester, Founder of the Creator Institute, who guided and mentored me this magnificent book experience. To the team at New Degree Press: Ashley Alverez and Jordana Megonigal, who pushed me to go deeper into the stories, Brian Bies who kept those deadlines rocking no matter what and giving weekly motivation tidbits to help push through, Ryan Porter, who stepped in giving support and direction in every step of the publishing process.

To Emma Marwood, Ms. Hardy, Mr. Crawford, Mr. Sparks, Ms. Dudley, Mr. Grier, Ms. Pope, Brandon Clokey, Yvonne Thayer, and Marissa McNamara, thank you for your mentorship, guidance, and support along the way.

To you, my dear beta-readers, thank you. This book has been a journey and you are now a part of it. I hope you share these lessons and stories as you allow your palates power to experience several of life's greatest exchange, sharing a meal and forming community and relationships around it.

Naomi Abraha

James Abyad

Soonhoon Ahn

Marie Alcero

Eva Anderson

Karen Anderson-Archer

Scott Aronson

Katherine Ashworth Brandt

Roland Austin

Riann Ballenger

Dr. Lisa Barber

Samantha Beard

Melvin Bell

Shirley Bennett Taylor

Roosevelt Bernard

Victor Betancourt

Meghan Bishop

Elizabeth Bland

Isabella Blecha

Juan Bordas

James Boyer

Thomas Bradley

Kimya Bradshaw

Adam Brown

Gavin Brown

Dr. Lara Brown

Amanda Bryson

Martin Burns

Carl Cabading

Jerry Cadely

Meg Calnan

Nicole Calvert

Marcus Cammack

Alex Cantone

Anna Catarina Levin

Lani Chau

Reginald "Reggie" Clark

Clair Clements

Brandon Clokey

Sydney Cole

Patricia Colon

Camille Colson

Peter Constantine

Dr. Michael Cornfield

Cynthia Coulange

Fernande Coulange

Phanol Coulange

Vanessa Coulange

Winfred Crawford

Anthony D'Andrea

Louis Dandridge

Layapole Davis

Andrew Doll

Anna Dove

Hansel Dsouza

Franchetta Dudley

Samuel Dupervil

Carole Edouard

CyEreka Edouard

Erick Edouard

Dr. Venita Edouard

Edidiong Ekasi-Otu

Tyriana Evans

Jean Exantus

Ilene Farley

Mackenzie Finklea

Eric Flior

Harry Francois

Esteban Fuentes

Marcelo Galdieri

Wanda Gamble

Reina Gascon-Lopez

Luce Gedeon

Robert Gedeon

Donna Gills

Yanique Gordon

Armando Gray Jr

Yves Gregoire Andre Francois

Michael Grier

Brianna Grooms

Wesley Grubb

Dynasty Hamilton

Sandra Hanna

Ravonda Hardy

Catherine Harrill

Kim Holden

Luevenia Holloway

Lindsey Holman

Chandler Hueth

Rodney Iler

Rachel Ingersoll

Monique Isaac

Wilzer Jean-Baptiste

Tonya Jennings

Evelyn Johnson

Merlon Jones

Merlon Jones Jr.

David King

Dana Klaboe

Eric Koester

Sydnee Koshar

Lauren Kuenstner

Jean Laguerre

Marie Lamothe

Tammy Le

Debbie Lei

Mildred LeJeune

Marie Lerch

Shannon Livingston

Kier Lofton

Luke Lorenz

Barbara Louisius

Benoit Louisius

Erick Louisius

Erick Louisius Jr.

Janice Louisius

Kettelye Louisius

Marie Louisius

Jessica Loyola

Elizabeth Luxama

Grace Maliska

Hans Manzke

Wilson D. Martinez

Emma Marwood

Tierney McDonnell

Ben McFarland

Marissa McGill

Marissa McNamara

Corinne Mercedes

Julie Mies

Charles Minder

Rachel Molnar

Christina Mondestin

Paula Morales

Linda Morency

Jordayne Moses

Lori Murphy

Joe Nelson

Julia Nista

Nadine Norgaisse

Daphnee Normil

Brooke Norwood-Vanzie

Angela Obie

Anisa Omar

Gretchen Ortega

Karla N. Pagan-Morales

Brittany Panetta

Malisa Payne

Tracy Pelt

Kristin Perkins

Cassandra Pittman

Veaceslav Pituscan

Jeannine Purvis

Lisa Ramirez

Lisa Rayam

Rultz Raymond

Michelle Risse

Rebecca Robinson

Madeline Rohrbacher

Courtney Rowe

Joshua Scherer

Kharina Scrubb

Latasha Seidu

Trina Shelton-Pope

Christina Shorter

Zacchaeus Shoulars

Lisa Shuler

Ted Sickley

Voltaire Silien

Susan Sloan

Lamanion Sparks

Sharon Spencer

Vivian Stephen

George Stone

Marcus Strickland

Katie Styles

Alissa Swango

Myrlande Taylor

Grace Terimbere

Blain Tesfaye

Ava Thek

Nicholas Tiernan

Roberto Umana

Jaynine Vado

Nikki Vonderhaar

Nadine Wheat

Rachele Willis

Dr. Allison Wimbush

Johnson Winfred

Renell Word

Carol Yee

Julie Yost

APPENDIX

INTRODUCTION

The Cambridge English Dictionary. s.v. "foodie (n.)." 2020. https://dictionary.cambridge.org/us/dictionary/english/foodie.

Child, Julia. "A Quote by Julia Child." Goodreads.com. 2020. https://www.goodreads.com/quotes/814094-people-who-love-to-eat-are-always-the-best-people.

"The Role of Food in Human Culture." Global Gastros. 2018. https://globalgastros.com/food-culture/role-of-food-in-human-culture.

Kennedy, John F. Pre-Presidential Papers. "Remarks at Corn Palace in Mitchell, South Dakota." September 22, 1960. https://www.jfklibrary.org/archives/other-resources/john-f-kennedy-speeches/mitchell-sd-19600922.

CHAPTER 1

Angelou, Maya. "BrainyQuote.com." BrainyMedia, Inc. 2020. https://www.brainyquote.com/quotes/maya_angelou_578828.

Kieff, Leah. "4 Foods You Must Try In Moldova." *Peacecorps.Gov.* December 10, 2015. https://www.peacecorps.gov/stories/4-foods-you-must-try-in-moldova/.

Pavarotti, Luciano. "Luciano Pavarotti Quotable Quote." *Goodreads, Inc.* 2020. https://www.goodreads.com/quotes/139486-one-of-the-very-nicest-things-about-life-is-the

"The Role of Food in Human Culture." *Global Gastros.* 2018. https:// globalgastros.com/food-culture/role-of-food-in-human-culture.

CHAPTER 2

Brillat-Savarin, Jean Anthelme. *BrainyQuote.com.* BrainyMedia, Inc. 2020. https://www.brainyquote.com/quotes/jean_ anthelme_brillatsav_374485.

Cachat, Dominique. "A guide to French Cuisine." Expatica. September 14, 2020. https://www.expatica.com/fr/lifestyle/food-drink/french-cuisine-104020/.

Chen, Vivian Hsueh-Hua. "Cultural Identity." *Key Concepts in Intercultural Dialogue* 22, no. 1.

"Evolution of Food Tourism." World Food Tourism. 2020. https:// worldfoodtravel.org/what-is-food-tourism/.

Miller, Siobhan, Ashley Peek. "5 Reasons Eating Will Always Be the Best Part about Traveling." *Her Campus Media LLC,* 2019. https://spoonuniversity.com/lifestyle/5-reasons-eating-will-always-be-the-best-part-about-traveling.

Monaco, Emily. "The French Influence on Vietnamese Cuisine." *Epicure & Culture.* December 16, 2015. https://epicureandculture.com/vietnamese-cuisine-french-influence/.

Wolf, Erik. "Culinary Tourism: A Tasty Economic Proposition." 2001. https://worldfoodtravel.org/what-is-food-tourism/.

CHAPTER 3

Allen, John S. The Omnivorous Mind: Our Evolving Relationship with Food. Harvard University Press. Cambridge, MA. 2012.

Paulemon, Kelly. "Soup Joumou - the Taste of Freedom." *VisitHaiti.* December 2018. https://visithaiti.com/food-drink/soup-joumou/

"Palate: Definition of Palate by Oxford Dictionary on Lexico.com Also Meaning of Palate." *Lexico Dictionaries English.* 2020. https://www.lexico.com/en/definition/palate.

"Power - Dictionary Definition." Vocabulary.com. 2020. https://www.vocabulary.com/dictionary/power.

CHAPTER 4

Gascon-Lopez, Reina. "Who Is Reina." *The Sofrito Project.* 2020. https://www.sofritoproject.com/about.

Lynn, Andrea. "What Defines Authentic Soul Food." *The Spruce Eats.* July, 3, 2020. https://www.thespruceeats.com/soul-food-history-and-definition-101709.

Satchmo's. "Ten Reasons Why We Love Brunch!" *Satchmo's Bar & Grill,* October 20, 2017. https://satchmosgrill.com/ten-reasons-why-we-love-brunch/

Schmidt, Diane. "How to Maintain Your Culture When Moving to Another Country." *The Spruce.* April 11, 2019. https://www.thespruce.com/maintain-your-culture-moving-another-country-2436103.

Shakespeare, William. *Hamlet, Prince of Denmark*. England: 1603. Act I, Scene 111, Line 564

Tolkien, John Ronald Reuel. *The Hobbit*. Boston: Houghton Mifflin, 2002.

Wolff, Anita. "Soul Food." *Encyclopedia Britannica*, February 14, 2020. https://www.britannica.com/topic/soul-food-cuisine.

CHAPTER 5

Beard, James. *BrainyQuote.com*, BrainyMedia, Inc, 2020. https://www.brainyquote.com/quotes/james_beard_140985.

Fayed, Saad. "Middle Eastern Social Mezze Meal." *The Spruce Eats*. March 14, 2019. https://www.thespruceeats.com/definition-of-mezze-2355566.

Garrett, Brianne. "Slutty Vegan Founder Pinky Cole Is 'Walking the Walk' with Her Justice Efforts." *Forbes*. July 2, 2020. https://www.forbes.com/sites/briannegarrett/2020/07/02/slutty-vegan-founder-pinky-cole-is-walking-the-walk-with-her-justice-efforts/#1d7a814211bd.

Hinderliter, Sandra. "Friends at the Lunch Table: Teaching Kids Empathy at School." *The Christian Science Monitor*. February 20, 2014. https://www.csmonitor.com/The-Culture/Family/Modern-Parenthood/2014/0220/Friends-at-the-lunch-table-teaching-kids-empathy-at-school.

Merriam-Webster.com Dictionary. s.v. "community." 2020. https://www.merriam-webster.com/dictionary/community.

"Out & About." *The Culinary Diplomacy Project*. October 2019. https://www.theculinarydiplomacyproject.org/out-and-about

Pfortmüller, Fabian. "What does "community" even mean? A definition attempt & conversation starter", *Medium*, September 20, 2017. https://medium.com/together-institute/what-does-community-even-mean-a-definition-attempt-conversation-starter-9b443fc523d0#:~:text=%E2%80%9CA%20feeling%20of%20fellowship%20with,I%20share%20with%20other%20people.

Robberecht, Liana. "Family-Style Dining: Bringing People and Food Together." *Media Edge Communications, Inc.* August 11, 2016. https://www.restobiz.ca/family-style-dining-bringing-people-food-together/#:~:text=There%20is%20no%20better%20way,feast%20brought%20in%20on%20platters.

"Slutty Vegan ATL." Roaming Hunger. 2020.https://roaminghunger.com/slutty-vegan-atl/

Solomon, Micah. "The Slutty Vegan: Young, African American Founder Pinky Cole's Wild Success with Playful Vegan Food." *Forbes*. July 12, 2019. https://www.forbes.com/sites/micahsolomon/2019/07/12/the-slutty-vegan-founder-pinky-cole-on-her-wild-success-bringing-playful-vegan-food-to-the-fore/#32de0c3314d8.

CHAPTER 6

Brunnstrom, David. "Kerry Visits Western-Leaning Moldova to Show Support." Reuters. December 4, 2013. https://www.reuters.com/article/uk-usa-moldova-kerry/kerry-visits-western-leaning-moldova-to-show-support-idUKBRE9B3OR020131204.

Beauchamp, Zack. "What You Need to Know about the Rwandan Genocide." *Vox,* April 10, 2014. https://www.vox.com/2014/4/10/5590646/rwandan-genocide-anniversary.

Chiu, Belinda, and Built Woo Commerce. "Mindful Diplomacy: The Case for Emotional Intelligence in Leadership." *Key Step Media.* 2020. https://www.keystepmedia.com/mindful-diplomacy-emotional-intelligence-leadership/.

Silverman, David J. "Thanksgiving Day." *Encyclopedia Britannica.* 2020. https://www.britannica.com/topic/Thanksgiving-Day.

"The Role of Food in Human Culture." *Global Gastros.* 2018. https://globalgastros.com/food-culture/role-of-food-in-human-culture.

CHAPTER 7

Agnew, Kelly Maia."7 Reasons Why It's Important to Explore New Food." Kelly Maia Nutrition. 2020.

"Everything You Know About Mexican Food Is A Lie." *Group Nine Media, Inc.* October 16, 2018. https://nowthisnews.com/videos/food/everything-you-know-about-mexican-food-is-a-lie.

Proverbs 18:21

Woolf, Virginia. *A Room of One's Own.* Boston: Mariner Books, 1989.

CHAPTER 8

Camden, Elizabeth. *Until the Dawn*. Bloomington, MN: Bethany House Publishers, 2015.

CHAPTER 9

Merriam-Webster.com Dictionary. s.v. "ambassador(n.)" 2020. https://www.merriam-webster.com/dictionary/ambassador.

Merriam-Webster.com Dictionary. s.v. "embassy (n.)" 2020. https://www.merriam-webster.com/dictionary/embassy.

Merriam-Webster.com Dictionary. s.v. "exchange(n.)" 2020. https://www.merriam-webster.com/dictionary/exchange.

Zhang, Ting. "Doing Business with China: Business Dinner Etiquette." *LinkedIn*. August 2, 2018. https://www.linkedin.com/pulse/doing-business-china-dinner-etiquette-ting-zhang/.

CHAPTER 10

Nigel Barber. "Why Some People Remember Events Better than Others." *Psychology Today*. October 22, 2019. https://www.psychologytoday.com/us/blog/the-human-beast/201910/why-some-people-remember-events-better-others.

Çelik, Doğan. "The Healing Effect of Gastrodiplomacy in Conflict-Affected Communities." *Policy* (2018).

Nye, Joseph S. "Soft Power: The Means to Success in World Politics." *Foreign Affairs Magazine*. May/June 2004. https://www.

foreignaffairs.com/reviews/capsule-review/2004-05-01/soft-power-means-success-world-politics.

Rockower, Paul S. "Recipes for Gastrodiplomacy." *Place Branding and Public Diplomacy* 8, no. 3 (2012).

Qin, Rong. "Diplomacy on the Dinner Table." *Diplomatic Courier.* March 30, 2019. https://www.diplomaticourier.com/posts/diplomacy-on-the-dinner-table

CHAPTER 11

Fieri, Guy. *BrainyQuote.com.* BrainyMedia, Inc. 2020. https://www.brainyquote.com/quotes/guy_fieri_797499

Team Unstoppable. "Oh What a Night!" *Unstoppable Foundation.* March 19, 2017. https://unstoppablefoundation.org/gala-magical-evening/.